# The Complete Guide to 1031 Exchanges, Private Equity & DST

*The Modern Investor's Blueprint for Passive Income*

*Updated for July 2025 Tax Laws!*

by
Lon Welsh
Author of *The Complete Guide to Passive Diversified Real Estate Investing*
Founder, IrontonCapital.com

Sean Ross
CEO, 1031x.com

For information to reproduce selections from this book, write to:

Permissions
Ironton Capital, LLC or 1031X.com
411 Walnut Street #23692
Green Cove Springs, FL 32043

First Edition

*Library of Congress Cataloguing-in-Publication Data*

ISBN 979-8-9907749-2-6

9798990774926

## *About the Authors*

**Lon Welsh** founded Ironton Capital, a private equity fund that helps investors achieve diversified passive income. He also founded Your Castle Real Estate, the largest independent brokerage in Colorado, with over 700 Real estate agents and 2,800+ transactions ($1.7 billion annually). He co-founded First Alliance Title, a top Colorado title company. A former strategic consultant with Deloitte, then Arthur Andersen (Accenture) for eight years, he has been a landlord for over 20 years, peaking at over 140 residential rentals. He then sold most of the residential to purchase commercial buildings.

He has been teaching investors for over 20 years on how to thrive with real estate investing. Lon has written over a dozen books including *The Colorado Guide to Real Estate Investing* and has created a lot of millionaires over that time.

While helping Real estate agents, their clients, and investors is Lon's passion, he has always found that true fulfillment comes from the familial bond with his team and fostering growth in the real estate community. Lon is a father of three, pursues travel, wine, painting, golf, tennis, running, and skiing in his free time. He serves on the boards and investment committees of the Denver Zoo, the Denver/Aurora Ronald McDonald House, and Denver Boys and Girls Club.

**Sean M. Ross** is the CEO of 1031x.com, Inc. ("1031X"), a top-rated national 1031 exchange qualified intermediary that has processed more than $7.5 billion in tax-deferred exchanges. With 31 years in operation and offices nationwide, 1031X performs exchange services in all 50 states.

Before joining 1031X, Sean's career spanned financial writing, business development, and investment consulting. He worked with Financial Poise in various roles, including Editor-in-Chief and Director of Business Development, and founded Free Lances Ltd., a professional ghostwriting service. Throughout his career as an investment advisor and consultant, Sean has bylined more than 2,000 articles covering tax, finance, investing, economics, and monetary theory.

Sean is affiliated with the Federation of Exchange Accommodators (FEA) and remains active in civic advocacy through volunteer work and financial support of the American Cancer Society and the Rocky Mountain MS Center. He holds a Bachelor of Science in economics and international political economy from Regis University. Sean enjoys travel, writing, meditation, weightlifting, and any team sport. He splits his time between Denver, CO, and Toronto, ON, with his wife and two children.

## *Selected Works Also by Lon Welsh*

*The Complete Guide to Passive Diversified Real Estate Investing, 2024*
Lon Welsh
Purchase on Amazon: irontoncapital.com/amazon

*How Real Estate Agents Can Succeed with AI: Streamline Your Business and Maximize Growth, 2024*
Lon Welsh, Joe Massey

*Thrive: How Real Estate Agents Can Succeed in Any Market, 2024*
Lon Welsh, Rick Davidson, Eric Flohr

*The Practical Guide to Colorado Real Estate Investing*
*5 Editions: 2018, 2016, 2013, 2011, 2009*
Lon Welsh, Charles Roberts, Greg Parham, Joe Massey

*Unlocked: Revealing the Eight Secrets of Highly Efficient Sales Professionals, 2012*
Darice Johnston, Lon Welsh, Bruce Gardner, Drew Shope

*The Real Estate IRA Retirement Planning Guide. 2012*
Jeff Sibel, with Lon Welsh and Charles Roberts

*Thrive: How Real estate agents Can Succeed in a Down Market, 2010*
Lon Welsh, Bruce Gardner, Mike Welk, Drew Shope

## *Meet the Authors Online*

### Lon Welsh

IrontonCapital.com
IrontonCapital.com/linkedin
IrontonCapital.com/facebook
IrontonCapital.com/youtube

### Sean Ross

1031x.com
LinkedIn.com/in/sean-m-ross-1031x/

## *What Our Investors Say*

*1031 Exchanges, Private Equity and DST* is an excellent resource for both seasoned investors and those newer to real estate. The authors have done a remarkable job of breaking down a highly technical and sometimes overwhelming subject into a clear, structured guide. The balance between practical checklists, real-world case studies, and deep dives into passive investment options makes the material both accessible and actionable.

What stands out most is the authors' combined expertise and their ability to blend theory with real-world experience. Lon Welsh's long track record in real estate and Sean Ross's leadership in 1031 exchanges shine through in the examples and nuanced insights. Their emphasis on diversification, pitfalls to avoid, and the role of building the right advisory team elevates this book beyond a "how-to" guide—it feels like a blueprint for long-term success. Overall, this is an invaluable contribution to the real estate investing community, and the authors should be commended for producing timely, thorough, and highly practical work.

- Joe Massey, Synergy One Lending

This book is thorough, practical, and well-structured, offering a strong balance between technical detail and accessible examples. It clearly positions 1031 exchanges alongside passive real estate strategies under new tax laws. It includes advanced concepts, such as reverse 1031 exchanges, and other opportunities for tax efficiency, such as cost segregation studies. Overall: credible, instructive, and quite useful for new as well as seasoned investors.

- Vital Aelion

Thirty-six years in the real estate industry and so much more to learn! *1031 Exchanges, Private Equity and DST* is full of investment structures and tax strategies which will maximize income potential. A must read for any savvy investor.

- Rick Davidson

Many real estate investors avoid 1031 exchanges due to the complexity and precision required to successfully take advantage of an exchange. However, these investors are leaving money on the table and missing out on a great wealth creation opportunity. Lon and Sean have written the perfect 'how to guide' to help investors identify and execute on a 1031 exchange. This book will be of great use to both new and experienced investors looking to create long-term wealth in real estate. The book explains 1031 exchanges, the trade-offs and options available to investors and the process of completing an exchange. I highly recommend this book to those looking to grow their real estate investments.

- Eric Flohr

Truly an excellent book, read very well for very sophisticated investors and not too difficult for a new one too :).

- Mike Zlotnick

As an active investor and real estate agent for over twenty years, I would highly recommend 1031 Exchanges, Private Equity and DST, to clients and colleagues. The book covers the spectrum from entry level basics to expert insight for seasoned real estate investors. I found the book useful as a refresher on exchanges, while gaining a deeper understanding on alternative opportunities for passive real estate income. Personally, it spurred an internal dialogue on key factors I need to evaluate to optimize my own portfolio. Further, I was very impressed in how topical the subject matter was, highlighting tax law changes from only two months ago. I'm keeping a copy of 1031 Exchanges, Private Equity and DST readily available to help guide myself and clients on purchasing and selling decisions, as well as overall portfolio management.

- Andrew Darlington, CRS

# Table of Contents

"In the middle of difficulty lies opportunity."
— Albert Einstein

"Teamwork is the fuel that allows common people to attain uncommon results."
— Andrew Carnegie

"If I have seen further, it is by standing on the shoulders of giants."
— Isaac Newton

We hope this book will help you make a great decision about what is likely one of your biggest investments. You'll need a team to get the optimal results. You can learn from the mistakes and insights of the investors that came before you. This will book will pull all of that together for you.

# Chapter 1:
# 1031 Exchange Essentials

If you've been investing in real estate for a while, you've probably heard about 1031 exchanges. Maybe you've even done one or two. But as more investors look to transition from active to passive real estate ownership—a trend that has grown tremendously – understanding the nuances of these exchanges becomes increasingly important. The tax laws that were passed in July 2025 also will impact your decision process. You can learn more about them in Appendix 3.

We'll start with the basics, then dig into some of the less obvious aspects that can make or break your exchange.

## The Fundamentals

A 1031 exchange, named after Section 1031 of the Internal Revenue Code, allows you to defer capital gains taxes when you sell investment property and reinvest the proceeds into other investment property. It's been around since 1921, though the rules have evolved considerably.

Who can use a 1031 exchange?

Pretty much any taxpaying entity that owns investment real estate—individuals, partnerships, LLCs, corporations, and trusts. The key requirement is that the property must be held for investment or business use, not as your personal residence or as inventory for sale.

The basic premise is straightforward. If you're continuing your investment in real estate, just in a different form or location, why should you pay tax on the transition? (Similar to how you can move money between investments in your IRA without triggering taxes).

## Core Components of Any 1031 Exchange

Every successful 1031 exchange rests on five fundamental pillars. Overlook any one of these, and your exchange fails, triggering the full tax bill you were trying to defer.

### 1. Like-Kind Property

1031 exchanges only work if you reinvest into "like-kind" property after you sell. At first glance, this strikes many investors as both vague and limiting. The fortunate reality is that, for real estate, "like-kind" is surprisingly broad. You're not matching property types—you're matching the *nature of the investment.* Any real property held for investment or business use can be exchanged for any other real property held for investment or business use.

This means:

- A shopping center can be exchanged for farmland
- An office building can be exchanged for a portfolio of rental houses
- A single rental property can be exchanged for a fractional interest in a much larger property [such as through a Delaware Statutory Trust (DST)]

The key, again, is that both properties must be investment or business property. Your personal residence doesn't qualify, nor does property you're holding primarily for resale (like a fix and flip, or newly built residential units).

This flexibility is what makes 1031 exchanges particularly useful for investors looking to restructure their portfolios. You're not locked into replacing apartments with apartments or retail with retail.

What's particularly interesting for investors transitioning to passive ownership is that tenant-in-common (TIC) interests and Delaware Statutory Trust (DST) interests qualify as like-kind to direct property ownership. This opens the door to exchanging your actively managed fourplex for a fractional interest in a $50 million apartment complex with professional management.

## 2. The Exchange Timeline

The IRS gives you exactly two time periods, and these are absolute.

**The 45-Day Identification Period:** Starting the day after you close on your sale, you have exactly 45 calendar days to identify potential replacement properties. This identification must be in writing, signed by you, and delivered to your qualified intermediary or another party to the transaction (but not someone acting as your agent).

You have three ways to identify:

- The 3-Property Rule: Identify up to three properties regardless of value
- The 200% Rule: Identify any number of properties if their combined fair market value doesn't exceed 200% of what you sold
- The 95% Rule: Identify any number of properties, but you must acquire 95% of what you identified (rarely used because it's so restrictive)

At 1031X, approximately 90% of the clients identify using the 3-property rule.

**The 180-Day Exchange Period:** You must close on your replacement property within 180 days of selling your original property, or by the due date of your tax return (including extensions) for the year of the sale, whichever comes first.

These deadlines are statutory carved into the tax code itself. No exceptions for holidays, weekends, illness, or "my attorney forgot." The only relief comes from presidentially declared disasters, and even that is limited.

## 3. The Qualified Intermediary (QI)

**Pivotal rule:** You cannot touch the money. Not for a day, not for an hour, not even for a minute. The moment you gain access to or control over the sale proceeds, your exchange is disqualified, and you will incur taxable income from the sale.

To get around this restriction, the modern 1031 exchange industry emerged. Companies that process exchanges and hold money on behalf of their clients are called Qualified Intermediaries (QIs).

The QI:

- Takes assignment of your sale contract
- Receives the funds from your buyer at closing
- Holds those funds in a segregated account
- Uses those funds to purchase your replacement property
- Transfers the replacement property to you

Think of the QI as a specialized escrow agent whose entire purpose is to stand between you and your money, preserving your ability to defer taxes.

The QI cannot be someone who has acted as your employee, attorney, accountant, investment advisor, or real estate agent within the two years before the exchange.

## 4. Trading Equal or Up

To defer all your taxes, you must follow two rules:

- **Equal or Up in Value**: Your replacement property (or properties—you can buy more than one) must be worth at least as much as your relinquished property
- **Equal or Up in Equity**: You must reinvest all your net proceeds

Let's break this down with real numbers.

**Example 1 - Full Deferral:**

- Sell property for: $1,000,000
- Existing mortgage: $300,000
- Net proceeds: $700,000
- Buy replacement for: $1,200,000
- New mortgage: $500,000
- Cash invested: $700,000
- Result: All taxes deferred

**Example 2 - Partial Deferral:**

- Sell property for: $1,000,000
- Existing mortgage: $300,000
- Net proceeds: $700,000
- Buy replacement for: $800,000
- New mortgage: $200,000
- Cash invested: $600,000

- Cash kept: $100,000
- Result: Tax owed on $100,000 "boot" plus $100,000 of debt relief

The second example illustrates "boot"—any value received that isn't like-kind property. Boot can be:

- Cash you don't reinvest
- Debt relief (if you don't replace the debt)
- Personal property received
- Non-qualifying property received

## 5. Same Taxpayer Requirement

This rule isn't really a rule. You won't find it referenced in the Internal Revenue Code or in the Treasury Regulations. It's more of a. practical necessity based on the structure of the law and the IRS' reporting requirements.

When you report a 1031 exchange to the IRS, you do so on **Form 8824**. This form must include both the property(ies) sold and the property(ies) acquired, and it can only be reported across one tax return. This makes it impossible to start a 1031 exchange with one taxpayer and complete it with another.

We'll revisit this in another section.

# Other Essential Concepts

## Holding Period Requirements

While the tax code doesn't specify a minimum holding period, the property must be held for investment or business use, not resale. The IRS looks at your intent. Factors they consider:

- How long you held the property
- Your purpose in acquiring it
- How you reported it on tax returns
- Whether you made improvements for resale or for rental
- Your historical pattern of property transactions

Most tax advisors recommend holding for at least a year to clearly establish investment intent, though shorter periods can work if you can document a change in circumstances or strategy.

For example, one of Sean's business partners (and one of the founders of 1031X) bought an office building in Denver through a 1031 exchange. After three months, a nearby hospital sent an agent to knock on his door. They wanted to buy his office building and turn it into a parking lot. The result? Sean's partner sold the property and did *another* 1031 exchange into a new office building a few doors down the road. Even though his holding period ended up being quite short (<4 months), his intent at the time of acquisition was for long-term business and investment use.

## What Constitutes "Investment Property"

Investment property comes in many forms. Some notable examples include:

- Rental properties (residential or commercial)
- Land held for appreciation
- Properties used in your trade or business
- Mineral rights, water rights, and growing crops
- Long-term leases (30+ years remaining)
- Some conservation easements
- DST (Delaware Statutory Trusts)

## What Doesn't Qualify:

- Your primary residence
- Second homes (unless they meet strict rental criteria)
- Property held primarily for sale (dealer property)
- Inventory or stock in trade
- Securities, bonds, or notes
- Partnership interests (such as membership interest in an LLC or a limited partner interest in a syndication)

We'll go over more detail on qualifying properties later in this chapter.

### The Mechanics of Title Transfer

In a 1031 exchange, the QI typically uses one of two methods for title transfer:

- **Direct Deeding:** When you sell, your buyer deeds directly to your replacement property seller, and the replacement property seller deeds directly to you. You never technically own the cash.
- **Sequential Deeding:** More common today, the QI takes title from you, transfers to your buyer, receives title from the replacement property seller, and transfers to you. This creates a cleaner paper trail.

## Partnership Complications and the Same Taxpayer Rule

This is where many exchanges run into trouble. The fundamental rule is simple but rigid: the taxpayer who sells the relinquished property must be the same taxpayer who acquires the replacement property. For individuals, this is straightforward. For partnerships and LLCs, it gets complex.

### Understanding the Same Taxpayer Rule

If ABC LLC owns your apartment building, then ABC LLC must be the buyer of the replacement property. You can't have ABC LLC sell and then have the individual members buy replacement properties. This seems logical, but it creates significant problems when partners want to go different directions.

Consider these common scenarios:

**Scenario A: The Partnership Continues.** If all partners agree to continue together, the partnership can execute a straightforward exchange. The partnership sells the old property and buys the new one. Simple.

**Scenario B: Partners Want to Split.** This is where it gets tricky. Some attempt to do a "drop and swap"—distributing property to partners before the sale so each can do their own exchange. The IRS has successfully challenged many of these, especially when:

- The distribution happens close to the sale
- There was a prearranged buyer
- The partners had already agreed to sell before distribution
- The property required unanimous consent to sell

**Scenario C: Some Partners Want Out.** If some partners want cash while others want to exchange, consider:

- Having the continuing partners buy out the departing ones before the sale
- Using special allocations (if your operating agreement allows) to allocate more cash to departing partners
- Having the partnership do the exchange, then redeeming departing partners' interests

## The Substance Over Form Doctrine

The IRS doesn't just look at the paperwork; they examine the substance of the transaction. In *Chase v. Commissioner*, partners received tenant-in-common interests two days before a sale. The court ruled this was really a partnership selling property, not individuals, denying 1031 treatment.

Key factors the IRS considers:

- How long property was held after distribution
- Whether sale negotiations began before distribution
- If the distributed property could realistically be held separately
- Whether business reasons existed for the distribution beyond tax avoidance

## Practical Partnership Strategies That Work

**Strategy 1: Long-Term Planning.** If partners might want to go separate ways, consider distributing properties or converting to tenant-in-common ownership well in advance—ideally at least a year before any sale.

**Strategy 2: Installment Sales to Partners.** A departing partner can sell their interest to remaining partners using an installment sale, spreading their tax burden while allowing others to exchange.

**Strategy 3: Partnership Continuation.** The partnership completes the exchange, acquiring multiple replacement properties. Later (after a reasonable holding period), the partnership distributes different properties to different partners.

## Special Considerations for LLCs

Single-member LLCs are generally disregarded for tax purposes, making exchanges straightforward. The member is treated as directly owning the property.

Multi-member LLCs face all the partnership complications unless they have elected corporate tax treatment. Even then, the corporation would need to do the exchange, not the shareholders.

Converting from a multi-member to a single-member LLC through buyouts beforehand can qualify for an exchange, but timing and documentation are crucial. The remaining member should have a real business purpose for the buyout beyond facilitating an exchange.

## A Tale of Two Exchanges: Real World Scenarios

Before we dive deeper into the mechanics, let's look at two scenarios that illustrate both the power and the pitfalls of 1031 exchanges.

### Scenario 1: The Denver Landlord's Transition

From 2008 to 2015, Mark and Jennifer acquired twelve rental properties in Denver's Highland neighborhood. By 2023, their portfolio had appreciated from $2.8 million to $7.2 million. They were both in their late 50s, tired of managing properties, and were concerned about Colorado's increasingly restrictive landlord-tenant laws.

**Their Challenge:** If they sold outright, they faced roughly $1.8 million in combined federal and state taxes. Here's how their exchange unfolded.

**Month 1:** They hired a qualified intermediary and listed their properties in three groups, timing the closings to happen within a 30-day window.

**Days 1-30:** The first group of properties closed, starting their exchange timeline. They had identified several Delaware Statutory Trusts (DSTs) offering fractional interests in institutional-grade properties: apartment complexes in Texas and Arizona, and a medical office portfolio in Florida. (We'll cover DST in more detail in Chapter 5, "DST in Depth".)

**Day 35:** With ten days left in their identification period, they formally identified six DST offerings totaling $7.5 million (staying under the 200% rule).

**Days 60-120:** As their remaining properties closed, they systematically invested the proceeds into four of the identified DSTs, ultimately placing $7.1 million.

**Result:** They transitioned from active management of 12 properties to passive ownership in professionally managed, institutional-quality real estate. Their monthly income increased due to better economies of scale, and they deferred the entire $1.8 million tax bill.

## Scenario 2: The Partnership Split Gone Wrong

The Patel and Singh families had been partners for 15 years, owning six apartment buildings through their LLC. When the Patels wanted to retire to Florida and the Singhs wanted to continue active investing, they attempted what seemed like a logical solution.

**The Failed Attempt:** Three months before listing the properties, they dissolved the LLC and distributed three buildings to each family. The plan was for each family to do their own 1031 exchange after the distribution.

**The Problem:** The IRS viewed this as a "disguised sale" of partnership interests. Under audit, they applied the "substance over form" doctrine, arguing that the true transaction was the Patels selling their partnership interest to the Singhs, not a property exchange. (Again, partnership interests do not qualify for 1031 treatment).

**The Costly Result:** The Patels' exchange was disqualified. They owed $680,000 in taxes they thought they'd deferred. The Singhs' exchange survived, but only after expensive legal battles.

**What Should Have Happened:** If they'd consulted proper tax counsel early, they could have either: (1) had the partnership itself do the exchange, then distributed interests in the replacement properties later, or (2) structured a buyout where the Singhs purchased the Patels' interest directly, allowing the Patels to invest their proceeds however they wished, including in a DST as passive investors.

## 1031 Exchange Timeline (and Checklist)

While there are (many) potential exceptions, the typical 1031 exchange follows a predictable timeline.

Here's a practical checklist for anyone considering a 1031 exchange.

**Before Listing Your Property:**

- [ ] Interview and select qualified intermediary (QI)
- [ ] Review your tax situation with your CPA
- [ ] Confirm the property qualifies (investment use, holding period)
- [ ] Consider timing for optimal tax year
- [ ] If partnership-owned, resolve structure issues

**At Contract Signing:**

- [ ] Notify QI immediately
- [ ] Include cooperation clause in sale contract
- [ ] Assign contract to QI if required

**Before Closing:**

- [ ] QI prepares exchange documentation
- [ ] Review and sign exchange agreement
- [ ] Confirm wiring instructions with QI
- [ ] Do NOT receive any funds directly

**Day 0 - Closing Day:**

- [ ] Funds wired directly to QI
- [ ] 45-day and 180-day calendars start tomorrow
- [ ] Begin property search immediately

**Days 1-40:**

- [ ] Actively search for replacement properties
- [ ] Get properties under contract if possible
- [ ] Line up financing if needed
- [ ] Leave buffer time before day 45

**By Day 45 (No Extensions!):**

- [ ] Submit written identification to QI
- [ ] Include complete addresses/legal descriptions
- [ ] Follow 3-property or 200% rule
- [ ] Keep copies of all identification documents

**Days 46-180:**

- [ ] Close on identified properties only
- [ ] Ensure QI sends funds directly to closing
- [ ] Do not take any cash to "round out" numbers
- [ ] Close before 180 days OR tax filing deadline

## Working With Qualified Intermediaries

It's unrealistic to expect real estate investors to be experts in 1031 exchange rules and procedures. The regulations are nuanced, full of exceptions, and frankly it is often quite dry and boring. That's why it's essential to rely on experts—it really falls upon each investor to find the right Qualified Intermediary who can navigate the process and ensure everything stays compliant.

A few practical considerations about QIs:

- They can't be someone who has worked for you in the past two years in an "agent" capacity (your attorney, CPA, real estate agent, financial advisor, etc.).
- Their fees typically range from $750 to $1,500 for a standard exchange.
- You want one that's financially stable and properly insured—QI failures, while rare, have happened.
- The QI's location often doesn't matter; 1031 rules are pleasantly consistent throughout the United States (with a few noteworthy exceptions, particularly when it comes to California).

When selecting a QI, ask about:

- Their insurance and bonding
- How exchange funds are held (segregated accounts are best)
- Their experience with your type of exchange
- Whether they're members of the Federation of Exchange Accommodators
- Their process for identifying properties and closing

## Understanding Basis and Depreciation

When you complete a 1031 exchange, your tax basis in the new property isn't its purchase price, it's essentially a continuation of your basis from the old property, with some adjustments. This has several implications.

Your depreciation schedule continues rather than resets. If you had $300,000 of remaining basis in your old property being depreciated over 15 years, that same schedule carries forward. Any additional basis from a larger replacement property starts its own depreciation schedule.

Let's look at a concrete example.

**Original Property:**

- Purchase price: $500,000 (10 years ago)
- Accumulated depreciation: $150,000
- Adjusted basis: $350,000
- Current value: $800,000

**Replacement Property:**

- Purchase price: $1,000,000
- Carryover basis: $350,000
- Additional basis: $200,000 (from new cash/debt)
- New total basis: $550,000

The $350,000 continues depreciating on the old schedule, while the $200,000 starts fresh. This continuation of basis is how the tax deferral works. You're not getting a stepped-up basis like you would in a regular purchase.

## Qualifying Properties: A Broader Definition Than You Might Think

Investment real estate obviously qualifies, but the definition extends beyond traditional rental properties.

- Tenant-in-common interests in larger properties
- Delaware Statutory Trusts (DSTs)
- Long-term leasehold interests (30+ years)
- Certain mineral rights and water rights
- Air rights and development rights (in some cases)
- Oil and gas royalty interests (in specific circumstances)
- Conservation easements (with careful structuring)

What doesn't qualify is generally property held for personal use or property held primarily for sale. That vacation home you rent out three months a year? Probably not, unless you've strictly limited your personal use according to Revenue Procedure 2008-16 (no more than 14 days or

10% of rental days, whichever is greater). This is a very tricky area to navigate. See your CPA!

Properties you're flipping? Generally no, as they're considered inventory rather than investment property. However, if your strategy changes and you decide to hold a flip as a rental for a reasonable period (typically at least a year), it may convert to investment property status. As with vacation homes, it's often difficult to think through edge cases with fix-n-flip projects.

## Common Pitfalls Worth Knowing About

1031x has seen tens of thousands of 1031 exchanges over the years. Over that time, certain mistakes appear repeatedly.

**Deadline misses:** Even sophisticated investors sometimes miscalculate the 45-day identification deadline. Remember, it's calendar days, not business days. Day 45 in our earlier example was a Sunday—identification had to be received by midnight Saturday.

**Identification errors:** Properties must be unambiguously identified. "A property in Denver" or even "A single-family condo in building XYZ" doesn't cut it. You need specific addresses or legal descriptions.

**Related party issues:** Exchanging with family members or controlled entities faces strict scrutiny and special rules. This is particularly true when buying property from a related party.

**Trying to just replace equity or gain:** A lot of investors mistakenly believe that they can defer all their taxes by simply reinvesting their equity (i.e. not replacing debt) or only reinvesting their capital gain. Each of these is a recipe for owing a lot more taxes than initially intended.

**State complications:** Some states don't fully conform to federal 1031 rules. California, for instance, has "clawback" provisions for California properties exchanged for out-of-state properties.

**Mixed-use properties:** If you've used part of a property personally (like a home with a rental unit), only the investment portion qualifies for exchange. Careful allocation is required.

## Practical Considerations

As you think about whether a 1031 exchange makes sense for your situation, consider both the immediate tax savings and your longer-term investment goals. The tax deferral can be substantial—often 30-40% of your gain when you factor in federal capital gains, state taxes, and depreciation recapture.

But the real power might be in what it enables: the ability to restructure your portfolio without the tax friction that normally comes with selling appreciated property. For investors looking to transition from active to passive ownership, this can be the tool that makes it economically feasible.

## Closing Thoughts

Here are some final thoughts as you consider your options:

**The Power of Deferral:** If you're 55 and deferred $500,000 in taxes, investing that money at even a modest return could mean an extra $1.2 million in wealth by retirement.

**The Step-Up Opportunity:** Hold exchanged property until death, and your heirs may receive a stepped-up basis, essentially erasing the deferred tax liability.

**The Flexibility Factor:** Today's exchange into active properties doesn't prevent tomorrow's exchange into passive investments. You can continue exchanging as your investment goals evolve.

**The Professional Team:** Successful exchanges require coordination between your QI, CPA, attorney, and real estate professionals. Assemble your team before you need them.

For 1031 exchange guidance, visit https://1031x.com

In the next chapter, we'll explore what many investors are discovering—that the true costs of active real estate investing extend well beyond the obvious expenses, and why even successful landlords are reevaluating their approach.

# Chapter 2:
# Passive Investment Options

When you sell an investment property and want to defer capital gains, you don't always have to buy and manage another building. Passive investing lets you put your money to work without handling tenants, repairs, or daily operations. Some options allow 1031 exchange deferral; others offer different tax advantages.

In this chapter, we'll cover six common passive real estate strategies.

1. **DSTs (Delaware Statutory Trusts)** — The most widespread 1031-eligible passive option.

2. **TICs (Tenancy in Common)** — A legacy 1031 structure still used in niche cases.

3. **REITs (Real Estate Investment Trusts)** — Simple, liquid, and tax-efficient for IRAs but not 1031-eligible.

4. **Passive LLCs or "Syndications"** — Flexible single-deal investments with strong tax benefits but no 1031 tax benefits.

5. **Opportunity Zones (OZ)** — Specialized syndications in designated communities with major long-term tax breaks.

6. **Private Placements (PP) & Fund of Funds (FOF)** — Diversified portfolios of passive real estate deals with strong depreciation benefits. Tax savings rival a 1031.

Each section explains how the structure works, when it qualifies for a 1031 exchange, and the key tradeoffs to consider. Finally, we summarize which option might best fit your goals.

Some of the choices are only available for accredited investors. That is someone who:

- Is single with an income over $200,000
- Has dual income with income over $300,000
- Has a net worth of $1,000,000 (not counting primary residence)

The SEC (Securities and Exchange Commission) is evaluating changes to make it easier to meet accreditation standards.

## 1. DSTs – The Most Visible Option

### What is a DST?

A Delaware Statutory Trust (DST) is a legal trust under Delaware law that owns real estate and is managed by a trust sponsor. By purchasing a share, you own part of a property without having to manage it yourself. (We'll cover DSTs more in depth in Chapter 5.)

Because DSTs follow IRS rules, you can use them for a 1031 exchange to defer capital gains taxes.

### How DSTs Work

1. A sponsor forms a DST and buys a property (such as an apartment complex or medical office).
2. Investors buy shares, giving them monthly income from rent.
3. The entire DST usually lasts 7–10 years before the property is sold.

## DST Benefits

- **Hands-off**: No tenant calls or repair coordination.
- **Lower Entry Point**: Some start at $50K–$100K.
- **Tax Deferral**: Use DSTs to defer paying capital gains—just like buying another active property.
- **Depreciation**: You get part of the tax benefit from depreciation.
- **Big Properties**: Access to large, well-maintained properties you might not afford otherwise.
- **Stable Income**: Many DSTs own buildings other than multifamily with long-term leases (5–20 years) that give steady rent.

## DST Drawbacks

- **No Control**: You can't choose the tenants or decide on repairs.
- **Illiquid**: You can't cash out before the trust ends—5 to 10 years is typical.
- **Fees**: Sponsors charge fees to buy and manage the trust.
- **Limited Strategy**: Sponsors can't change strategy—it's passive only. Value-Add and Development projects are not compatible with DST rules.
- **Market Risk**: If property values fall, your investment value goes down too.

### DST Performance

- Typical cash-on-cash returns are 5–9% per year.
- Additional gains can come when the building is sold.
- In general, total returns around 10% are likely.

## 2. Tenancy-in-Common (TIC)

Before the rise of Delaware Statutory Trusts (DSTs), the most common way to co-own institutional-quality real estate as a 1031 investor was through a Tenant-in-Common (TIC) structure. While less common today, TICs are still used in certain situations, particularly for custom group deals or legacy investments.

### What is a TIC?

A TIC is a legal structure where up to 35 individual investors can each own a fractional interest in a single piece of real estate. Each investor holds direct title to their share, and the group collectively owns the property.

### How It Works:

- Each TIC owner is on title for their pro-rata share.
- Investors split income, expenses, and depreciation proportionally.
- Major decisions typically require unanimous or near-unanimous consent.
- A sponsor or asset manager often coordinates operations but does not have discretionary control.

**Benefits:**

- **1031-Eligible**: TIC interests qualify as "like-kind" for 1031 exchanges.
- **Control**: Owners may have more say in operations or sale decisions than in a DST.
- **Custom Structuring**: Often used when a small group of known investors wants to co-invest.

**Drawbacks:**

- **Unanimity Required**: Decision-making can become gridlocked.
- **Financing Limitations**: Lenders may hesitate to finance TICs due to fragmented ownership. Many or all investors might need to personally guarantee the loan. If you can find a lender that will do a non-recourse loan, it will usually involve less leverage (thus a lower return percentage) and/or higher rate.
- **Liquidity Challenges**: Selling a fractional TIC interest is nearly impossible.
- **Very Complex 1031 Exits**: Coordinated timing is required for all parties in future exchanges.

**When Are TICs Still Used?**

TICs remain a viable option for:

- Smaller groups of friends/family co-investing
- Deals requiring owner voting rights (e.g., development risk)
- Legacy portfolios that are still in TIC form

For most passive investors today, DSTs offer simpler management, less friction in financing, and broader access to institutional-grade real estate.

But knowing what a TIC is—and how it fits in—rounds out your understanding of the full passive investing landscape.

## 3. REITs (Real Estate Investment Trusts)

A Real Estate Investment Trust (REIT) is a company that owns, operates, or finances income-producing real estate. Most REITs are publicly traded on stock exchanges and function more like mutual funds than direct property investments.

### What Is a REIT?

A REIT pools investor capital to buy and manage portfolios of real estate: typically, commercial properties like apartments, office buildings, warehouses, or retail centers. Investors buy shares in the REIT, not the underlying real estate.

### How It Works:

- Investors purchase shares in a REIT through a brokerage (public) or offering platform (private).
- The REIT collects rent and distributes taxable dividends to shareholders.
- REITs must pay out at least 90% of taxable income to retain their tax-advantaged status.
- Most REITs are not 1031-eligible—but some private REITs or UPREIT structures may allow deferral options in limited cases.

**Benefits:**

- **High Liquidity**: Shares can be bought and sold daily (public REITs).
- **Diversification**: REITs typically own dozens or hundreds of properties.
- **Low Minimums**: Entry costs are typically far lower than other real estate investments.
- **Simplicity**: No management, paperwork, or property-specific risks.
- **Lower Risk**: Many REITs invest in lower risk strategies (e.g., Buy and Hold vs. Value-Add or Development). This tends to be the lowest risk form of real estate investing.

**Drawbacks:**

- **No 1031 Eligibility**: Public REIT shares do not qualify for tax deferral through 1031 exchanges.
- **Market Volatility**: Prices fluctuate with stock market sentiment, not just real estate performance.
- **Taxable Dividends**: Most payouts are fully taxable as ordinary income. Check with your CPA, sometimes there are some preferred tax rates for REITs.
- **Limited Control**: Investors cannot influence property selection or strategy.
- **No Losses**: Depreciation and other write-offs cannot be passed on to investors. If you are investing in your IRA, that doesn't matter. If you are trying to offset gains from the sale of an active or passive investment, this might be a lost opportunity. Check with your CPA.
- **Lower Return**: Many REITs invest in lower risk strategies.

### When Are REITs Useful?

REITs are a convenient option for:

- Investors who want real estate exposure in a retirement account or brokerage portfolio.
- Those who are prioritizing liquidity and simplicity over tax deferral or customization.
- People who are exiting real estate entirely and reallocating into a diversified, passive vehicle. If you don't need tax losses, this can be a nice alternative.

While REITs don't offer the tax-deferral benefits of 1031-friendly structures like DSTs or TICs, they remain a useful tool—especially for investors more focused on income and liquidity than tax efficiency.

## 4. Passive LLCs or "Syndication"

A Passive LLC investment involves joining a limited liability company that owns and operates one or more real estate properties. These deals are often smaller and more flexible than institutional funds and are frequently used for one-off projects. We cover Syndications (also known as "Private Placements") in depth in Chapter 6.

### What Is a Passive LLC?

In this structure, you invest capital into an LLC managed by a sponsor or general partner (GP). The GP controls acquisition, operations, and exit strategy, while you participate as a limited partner (LP). This entitles you to a share of the income, depreciation, and profits, but with no management control.

## How It Works:

- You invest a set amount (often $50K–$500K) into the LLC.
- The LLC owns the real estate asset(s) and handles all decision-making.
- Cash flow is distributed based on ownership shares, and tax benefits flow through via K-1s.
- Most are not 1031-eligible, but in some cases (e.g., with special structuring or a TIC setup) a 1031 exchange may be possible.

## Advantages:

- **Passive Ownership**: No landlord responsibilities or asset management required.
- **Strong Tax Benefits**: Depreciation and cost segregation can offset other gains (such as the capital gains due from the sale of an investment property).
- **Custom Structuring**: Sponsors may design the deal around investor goals.
- **Transparency**: Smaller scale allows more direct communication with the sponsor.

## Drawbacks:

- **Limited Liquidity**: These are typically long-term, illiquid investments (3–7 years).
- **No 1031 Exchange by Default**: Most LLC interests do **not** qualify for 1031 unless structured specifically (e.g., TIC).
- **Sponsor Risk**: You rely heavily on the GP's judgment and execution.

- **Smaller Scale**: Fewer properties means higher concentration risk.

### When Are Passive LLCs Useful?

This structure works well for:

- Investors who want to stay passive but still pick (and prefer) individual deals or markets.
- Those seeking customized, direct exposure without the scale of a full fund.
- Investors looking to use depreciation to offset gains while avoiding operational involvement.

Passive LLCs are a foundational tool in private real estate and often serve as the building blocks for larger funds or roll-up strategies. They bridge the gap between DIY real estate and full institutional offerings.

## 5. Opportunity Zones (OZ)

An OZ fund is a Qualified Opportunity Fund (QOF) that is set up as a corporation or partnership specifically to invest at least 90% of its assets into eligible properties within economically distressed areas known as Opportunity Zones. In structure, it functions much like a real estate syndication—you invest as a limited partner while a sponsor (general partner) manages the deal. But unlike traditional syndications, OZ funds must follow IRS-defined rules in exchange for extraordinary tax incentives. We cover OZ in depth in Chapter 7.

Opportunity Zones (OZs) were created to spur investment in designated low-income communities. OZ investments are limited to properties or businesses within specially designated census tracts.

### What Is an OZ Fund?

An OZ fund is a Qualified Opportunity Fund (QOF) that pools investor capital to buy or develop real estate or businesses in Opportunity Zones—geographic areas identified by each state and approved by the federal government.

### How It Works:

- You must invest capital gains (not ordinary income) into a QOF within 180 days of recognizing the gain.
- The fund then invests that money into qualifying OZ property or businesses.
- If held for 5 years, a portion of the original gain is forgiven.
- If held for 10+ years, all appreciation on the OZ investment is 100% tax-free under current rules.

### Advantages:

- **Significant Tax Deferral**: Capital gains can be deferred for up to five years under the new 2025 tax law.
- **Partial Forgiveness**: 10% of original gains are permanently excluded after five years (30% for rural OZ funds).
- **Tax-Free Growth**: If you hold the OZ investment for 10+ years, the growth is entirely tax-free.
- **Potential for Impact**: Investments support underdeveloped communities.
- **Great Plan B** if your 1031 exchange fails. The 180-day window for the OZ doesn't begin until you get your funds (after 1031 fails).

**Drawbacks:**

- **Strict Rules**: Must follow detailed IRS regulations on timing, property type, and reporting.
- **Limited Availability**: Only projects in approved zones qualify—some zones may not offer strong fundamentals.
- **No Ordinary Income Allowed**: Only capital gains can be contributed.
- **Illiquidity**: Like other private placements, OZ funds are long-term, non-traded investments.

**When Are OZs Useful?**

OZs are ideal for:

- Investors with large capital gains looking to reduce or eliminate future tax liability.
- Those seeking a long-term hold (10+ years) with significant after-tax upside.
- Individuals interested in aligning tax strategies with social impact.

## 6. Private Placements & Fund of Funds

Private Placements (PP) are a widespread way for accredited investors to passively participate in real estate—typically through limited partnerships or LLCs. These offerings are not publicly traded and often focus on a single asset (like a multifamily property or self-storage facility) or a small portfolio of related properties. Investors contribute capital as limited partners, while a sponsor or general partner manages the project. These investments are usually not 1031-eligible, but they offer strong tax benefits through depreciation, cost segregation, and creative deal structuring. With the tax benefits, you can often "synthetically" re-create the tax situation of a 1031 exchange.

Some firms—like Ironton Capital—offer a Fund of Funds (FOF) which is a diversified private placement fund, where investor capital is pooled and then deployed across a curated mix of underlying deals. These FOF structures aim to reduce risk through sponsor and asset diversification, while still offering tax benefits and attractive projected returns. We cover PP and FOF in depth in Chapter 6.

### What They Are

These are private deals sold to accredited investors.

- A private placement usually means investment in one property (like one warehouse).
- An FOF pools several properties under one plan—perhaps a mix of warehouses or apartments.

### Private Placement vs. Syndication: What's the Difference?

A Private Placement refers to the regulatory structure—an offering of securities (like equity or debt) to a limited number of accredited investors under exemptions from SEC registration, typically under Regulation D.

A Syndication, on the other hand, is a type of private placement where investors pool money to buy a specific real estate asset, like a single apartment building or self-storage facility.

### How It Works

1. You commit money (often $50K+).
2. The sponsor buys and manages properties, perhaps repairing or repositioning them. This is a higher risk, higher reward strategy than the very conservative strategies in most DSTs and REITs.
3. You often get monthly or quarterly income and a larger payout at sale (the "exit").

### Benefits

- **Higher Target Returns**: Often 12–20% IRR (Internal Rate of Return) for overall profits. IRR combines income and growth into a single rate.
- **More Tax Breaks**: Sponsors use cost segregation to break property into parts, speeding up depreciation to save taxes earlier.
- **Growth Potential**: Sponsors may improve rents or sell at a higher price due to value-added renovations.
- **Depreciation Helps**: You may even offset some capital gains from earlier sales of your investment properties (or appreciated stocks).

### Drawbacks

- **More Risk**: Often (not always) not tied to long-term leases.
- **Long Lock-up**: 5–7 years is typical.
- **High Fees**: Funds charge for managing and performance.
- **Only for Accredited Investors**: Not open to everyone under SEC rules.

# Comparison Grid

In Figure 2-1 you'll find a chart comparing the six different passive investment options.

| Feature | DST | TIC | REIT | Passive LLC / Syndication | OZ Fund | Private Placement / Fund of Funds |
|---|---|---|---|---|---|---|
| 1031 Eligible | ☑ Yes | ☑ Yes | ✖ No (with exceptions) | ✖ Usually not | ✖ Not for original gain | ✖ Usually not |
| Minimum Investment | $50K–$100K | $100K+ (often higher) | <$1K (public REITs) | $50K–$500K | $50K+ | $50K+ |
| Investor Role | 100% Passive | Semi-active (voting) | 100% Passive | 100% Passive | 100% Passive | 100% Passive |
| Liquidity | ✖ Illiquid (7–10 yrs) | ✖ Very illiquid | ☑ High (public REITs) | ✖ Illiquid (3–7 yrs) | ✖ Illiquid (10+ yrs) | ✖ Illiquid (5–7 yrs) |
| Depreciation Benefit | ☑ Yes (via K-1) | ☑ Yes | ✖ Not passed to investor | ☑ Yes | ☑ Yes | ☑ Yes |
| Control / Voting | ✖ None | ☑ Some (often unanimous) | ✖ None | ✖ None | ✖ None | ✖ None |
| Target Returns (IRR) | 6–10% (pre-tax) | 6–10% (pre-tax) | 5–8% (pre-tax) | 10–18% (pre-tax) | 10–12% (after-tax) | 12–20% (pre-tax) |
| Tax Deferral Strategy | 1031 | 1031 | Usually None (unless UPREIT) | "Synthetic 1031" via depreciation | OZ Tax Benefits | "Synthetic 1031" via depreciation |
| Risk Level | Low-Moderate | Low-High | Lowest | Moderate–High | Moderate–High | Moderate–High |
| Best For | Simple deferral + income | Group control + 1031 | Liquidity + simplicity | Custom projects w/ tax shelter | Big gains + tax-free growth | Big gains + possible tax shelter |
| Headache | Likely lowest returns | Complex to set up; loan guarantee | Likely lowest returns | Up-front tax planning is more work | 10 years to max tax benefits | Up-front tax planning is more work |

**Figure 2-1: Comparison Chart**

## Closing Thoughts

Choosing the right passive real estate investment depends on your goals, risk tolerance, liquidity needs, and tax strategy. Here's a recap to help you decide.

**If you want…**

- Steady Income with Low Involvement: Consider a **DST**. It's the easiest option for 1031 investors who want predictable cash flow and zero management responsibility. If wealth preservation is more important than growing your wealth, this is likely for you.

- Some Control and Co-Ownership: A **TIC** may work if you're investing with known partners and want voting rights, though it comes with more complexity. Be aware of the risks of guaranteeing a loan.

- High Liquidity and Simplicity: **Public REITs** provide stock-like flexibility and instant diversification—best for retirement accounts or when 1031 deferral isn't needed. Like the DST, this choice is more about limited asset growth and more about wealth preservation.

- Customization and Tax Benefits: A **Passive LLC or Syndication** gives you direct access to individual deals often with strong depreciation benefits, but usually without 1031 eligibility. The lack of diversification increases risk.

- Long-Term, Tax-Free Growth Potential: An **Opportunity Zone Fund** offers powerful incentives if you've realized a large capital gain and can commit for 10+ years. Note the ROI (return on investment) will be lower due to no refinance allowed in the hold period. Best for wealth preservation and/or when you have a lot of tax to shield.

- **<u>Diversification with Higher Upside</u>**: A **Private Placement** or **Fund of Funds** (like those offered by Ironton Capital) spreads your investment across many deals while offering accelerated depreciation and higher target returns—ideal if you don't need liquidity. If you still want to grow your wealth and manage taxes, this could be a good fit. To see if Passive Investing in a Fund of Funds is right for you, choose your time to speak to one of Ironton Capital's investor relations team at irontoncapital.com/gopassive

Each option serves a distinct purpose. Your ideal path might involve combining a few of these tools to match short-term needs and long-term goals.

# Chapter 3: The Hidden Costs of Active Real Estate Investing

Chapter 2 introduced you to the 1031 exchange fundamentals. Now that we understand the landscape, let's look at some evaluation criteria you will want to consider.

In certain markets and phases of the real estate cycle, active real estate investment can reward an investor's time with additional return. Often these extra returns are relatively easy to calculate. You can take the surplus returns from active management, subtract the return from an easier passive investment, and determine how much they are getting paid for the extra work and risk.

This is a calculation you or your financial team should perform as you sell one active asset and explore your options. Your projections may never be perfectly accurate but having even an approximation can really improve your decision-making. Consider estimating how many hours you'd invest in the active project to calculate your dollar per hour earned. It might be eye-opening!

The choice between active and passive real estate investments has more dimensions than purely ROI (return on investment) and sweat-equity return. This chapter explores eight other considerations you should evaluate for a well-rounded decision. Some are quantitative and some are qualitative.

1. **Time, Stress & Opportunity Costs**

    - Landlord time commitment and emotional burden (e.g., tenant issues, compliance stress).
    - The six passive investing strategies identified in Chapter 2 shift management burdens to sponsors: freeing up time and mental energy.

2. **The Landlord Burden in Different Markets**

    - Hidden costs that are not immediately obvious (for example, maintenance, vacancies, and insurance) can erode returns.
    - Private equity funds and DST handle these activities centrally, delivering economies of scale and with no effort for investors.

3. **When Active Investing Stops Making Sense**

    - Sometimes markets (e.g., Austin, as of 2025) or assets classes (e.g., office) underperform.
    - Trade-offs: You could complete a 1031 exchange into a replacement. Often, paying capital gains to enter a high-yield passive fund makes more sense—higher net IRR, less hassle.

4. **Concentration Risk (Lack of Diversification)**

    - There can be dangers in being tied to one asset, market, or sponsor.
    - A 1031 exchange or passive investing can spread risk across sponsors, geographies and asset types. Diversification reduces exposure to individual-market volatility.

## 5. Common Pitfalls & How to Avoid Them

- Common errors of active managers include under-capitalization, poor tenant screening, overleveraging, and refinancing risk in DST structures (e.g., DSTs can't refinance, which can be a major strategic blind spot).
- Private equity funds can mitigate these pitfalls, particularly through sponsor-led underwriting, reserve planning, and depreciation strategies.

## 6. Tax Efficiency Beyond Deferral

- A 1031 exchange to another active rental often results in the best tax outcome but might not optimize after-tax returns.
- A DST is usually the path of least resistance—with minimal hassle and strong tax efficiencies—but usually delivers the lowest after-tax returns over time.
- A private equity investment may be less tax efficient but provide the best after-tax returns over time. Depreciation in the fund can offset realized gains—dramatically improving after-tax IRR.

## 7. Liquidity and Lock-Up Nuances

- A 1031 exchange for an active investment will usually maximize your choices of when and how to liquidate.
- Most other passive strategies (other than public REITs) are liquid only on sponsor timelines (typically 5–10 years).

8. **Sponsor Accountability and Alignment**

    - A 1031 exchange for an active investment will clearly have superior accountability to other options.
    - The six passive investing strategies have different levels of Sponsor / Manager alignment.

Let's explore each of these in turn.

# 1. Time, Stress & Opportunity Costs

Being an active real estate investor—especially a landlord—can feel rewarding, but it comes with hidden burdens.

**It Takes Time—and That Is Opportunity Cost**

If you manage rental properties yourself, you'll spend hours handling tenant calls, fixing broken heaters, filing paperwork, finding new renters, and more. Self-managing rentals can quickly eat away at your profits and peace of mind. Often it causes stress for the spouse of the primary investor.

That time could be spent doing other things—focusing on your primary job, being with family, doing volunteer work, or researching better investments. This is opportunity cost—what you lose by not doing something else.

Hiring a property manager will greatly reduce but not eliminate this burden. You'll still need to supervise them and check their work. Be sure that your active investment earns enough of a premium over the passive choice to properly reimburse you for this effort.

The six passive strategies described later chapters will require very little work by comparison.

### Emotional and Mental Stress

Tenants don't always pay rent on time. They might degrade your property, fight with other tenants, or violate lease rules. The stress can snowball—5 a.m. drama calls, repair emergencies, and legal headaches.

You also face regulations in every market, such as landlord-tenant laws, safety inspections, and eviction rules.

But when you go passive, a sponsor handles everything. Sponsors have teams for leasing, maintenance, compliance, and emergencies. That shields you from stress and leaves you with more peace of mind. They typically have sufficient scale to either maintain control or have special access to property management specialists.

### Example—Imagine Your Weekend

- **Active Landlord**: Saturday morning drain a flooded basement; Saturday afternoon switch broken locks; Saturday evening screen tenants.

- **Passive Investor**: Saturday morning relax with family or golf.

This is the time and emotional freedom passive strategies can unlock.

### The Real Trade-Off

Being active might give you higher returns when everything goes well. But you pay with your time, your energy, and your personal bandwidth. You might easily manage it today, but if something happens to your health (or if you must relocate for your job), do you have a plan B?

## 2. The Landlord Burden in Different Markets

Owning rental properties may look simple from the outside, but many hidden costs lurk just beneath the surface. These expenses can eat into profits and turn what seems like passive income into unwelcome surprises.

### Insurance and Taxes

Landlords need special insurance—not regular homeowners' coverage. This is often **25% more expensive**, and it should cover things like lost rent during repairs and injuries to the property.

Rental properties don't usually qualify for the typical homeowner tax benefits, which means you'll often pay higher property taxes. This tends to occur even more frequently with short-term rentals.

### Maintenance and Emergency Repairs

You might choose to get a NNN (triple net) property where the tenant is responsible for maintenance. This is common with industrial and retail investments. DSTs usually focus on this investment type.

For many other asset classes, the owner is responsible for repairs—both the cost, coordination and oversight. Routine upkeep like lawn care or repainting is just the start. Big-ticket repairs like fixing pipes, installing a new HVAC system, or repairing roofs can quickly drain your bank account. Budgeting is challenging, since you never know when things will break.

### Vacancies & Turnover

Every time a tenant leaves you lose rent, and you often must pay a leasing fee to find a new one. While the unit is empty, you still pay the mortgage, taxes, and utilities.

**Tenant Damage & Compliance**

Unfortunately, some tenants may trash the place. This is most common with residential assets, less so with the others (like industrial). Repairs beyond the security deposit mean out-of-pocket costs.

**Regulatory Compliance**

Missing a local safety rule or lease update could lead to legal penalties. In the Colorado market, nearly a dozen new laws were passed in 2023-2025. All of them were to the benefit of the tenant, at the expense of the landlord. It is now much more difficult to evict a tenant, or even non-renew a troublesome tenant.

## 3. When Active Investing Stops Making Sense

Active real estate investment can pay off, especially in strong markets. An active strategy might make more sense in some phases of the market cycle than others. But conditions change. A property type or local market that once performed well can suddenly underperform. Recognizing when to shift gears is important—that's where 1031 exchanges and passive investing can offer real value.

**Markets That Turn Against You**

Office buildings are a top example. Before COVID, offices were strong investments. But when remote and hybrid work styles persisted, office vacancies surged. U.S. office supply remained oversupplied, and office values dropped sharply. Some submarkets in 2025 are still below pre-pandemic occupancy levels.

Even as the sector recovers—leasing is slowly climbing in cities like San Francisco—levels are nowhere near pre-pandemic occupancy. Though investors have re-entered the market, recovery may take years—and continued risk remains.

**When the Strategy No Longer Delivers**

Active strategies like buy-and-hold or value-add depend on market strength. But when markets turn, these approaches can fail you.

- **Buy & Hold**: Relying on stable rent and occupancy can backfire if demand drops.
- **Value-Add or Development**: High-leverage projects that depend on market growth become risky if leasing stalls.

A recent MSCI study highlighted that office values dropped over 40% between 2020 and 2025, and multifamily saw 20-22% declines. (See Figure 3-1)

Index: 100 – 2007 average price / SF.

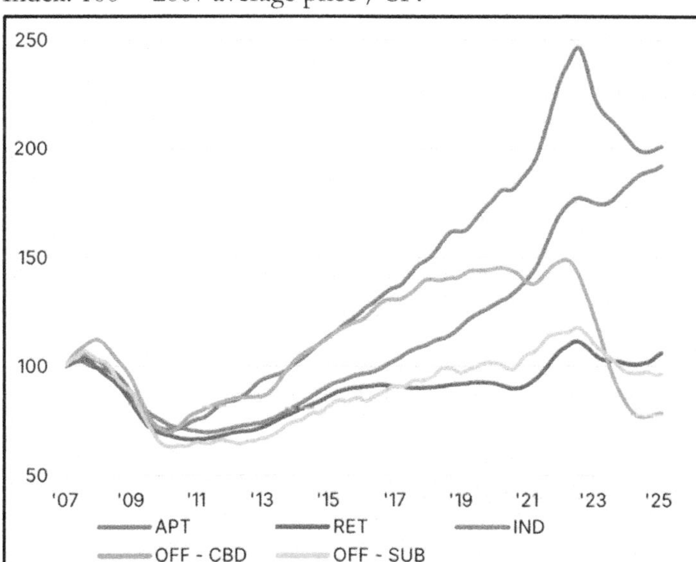


*Source: MSCI*

**Figure 3-1 Commercial Real Estate Prices by Asset Class**

## 4. Concentration Risk (Lack of Diversification)

Have you ever heard the saying *"Don't put all your eggs in one basket"*? That's exactly what concentration risk means. Concentration risk happens when you invest too heavily in one thing. When too much of your real estate investments are tied to one thing—like a single property, market, or sponsor—you risk everything if it goes wrong.

For example:

- Owning many units in just one city.
- Putting all your money into one asset class (e.g., office).
- Focusing on just one strategy (e.g., Buy and Hold) vs. multiple strategies (e.g., adding some Value Add and/or Development)
- Investing only with one general partner (GP).

When that one thing drops in value, your whole portfolio takes a hit. Financial experts say that concentration risk is the chance that amplified losses happen if you rely too much on one asset or sector.

**Real-Life Example**

Imagine buying ten rental buildings in the same town with the same sponsor. You think you're diversified. But if the local economy crashes, the laws/regulations change, or the sponsor makes mistakes (like choosing the wrong property manager), *all ten properties* could struggle. That's a scary level of risk.

**The Danger of One Sponsor**

Often, active investors act as their own sponsor. That means every time you make a mistake, it might be repeated across many of your properties. Any misstep can affect everything.

An even more common risk: passive investors who rely on a single DST or sponsor. If that sponsor uses the wrong management team or makes a bad decision, *all of your investment* could suffer.

### How to Reduce Concentration Risk

#### Use a 1031 Exchange

A 1031 exchange lets you spread your capital over multiple properties in different markets or asset types. You maintain tax deferral while reducing risk.

#### Choose Multiple Passive Investments

Passive investing through several sponsors brings diversification. DSTs and REITS, for example, allow fractional ownership across different asset types and locations. This helps avoid leaning too heavily on one manager. Most Fund of Funds will as well.

#### Pay Taxes and Use Private Equity Funds

Some investors pay capital gains and invest in a private equity fund like Ironton Capital's. These funds often offer:

- Multiple sponsor teams working together
- Investments across different markets and asset types
- More dependable returns, even after taxes

This method helps protect against any single sponsor's mistakes and often offers better returns.

## 5. Common Pitfalls & How to Avoid Them

Here are the most frequent mistakes and how passive or partially passive strategies can help you avoid them.

### 1. Undercapitalization—Running Out of Money

You buy a property and don't leave enough money aside for repairs, maintenance, or unexpected expenses. Suddenly, a leaky roof or broken furnace shows up—and you're scrambling for cash.

**Why It's Common:** Everyone loves optimistic projections. But not setting aside a cushion—or worse, depending on future profits—can leave you financially exposed.

**How to Avoid It:** Consider budgeting *at least* 1–4% of the property's value per year for upkeep and have extra for major repairs. A private equity fund, managed well, groups reserves across many properties, so those costs don't fall on just you.

### 2. Poor Tenant Screening

You rent out a unit without checking income, credit, or past rental history—and the tenant turns out to be a late payer, property destroyer, or legal troublemaker. In some states, you may be legally limited in performing this research on tenant prospects.

**Why It's Common:** It is easy to skip checking references—especially if someone seems nice or offers more rent.

**How to Avoid It:** Do background and income checks every time if legally possible. Even simple protections, like lease clauses spelling out fines for damage, go a long way. Private sponsors manage these tasks professionally, keeping issues from spreading.

### 3. Overleveraging

You finance most of your deal—thinking higher leverage equals higher return—without enough buffer. Rising rates or a drop in rent can suddenly make payments unsustainable.

**Why It's Common:** Many investors borrow heavily expecting rents and values to keep rising.

**How to Avoid It:** Stick to lower debt-to-income ratios—under 65%—and run scenarios with rate rises. Private funds follow conservative underwriting, so you're not squeezed if something changes suddenly.

## 4. Refinancing Risk in DST and OZ—Locked In

After a 1031 exchange, DST and OZ investors often can't refinance. That matters when rates fall or properties need upgrades, and they can't pull out equity.

**Why It's Common:** DST and OZ are often built with fixed plans. There's no flexibility to refinance, so investors may miss chances to improve returns.

**How to Avoid It:** Using a 1031 into an actively managed private equity fund is an alternative. Sponsors can refinance when opportunities arise, improving cash flow or funding new projects.

## 5. Poor Exit Strategy—Trapped In

You invest expecting to hold long-term but later find you need liquidity. No buyers, no refinancing, and sale values could be much lower than your expected exit.

**Why It's Common:** Many investors get caught up in the rush to closing and forget to plan ahead.

**How to Avoid It:** Always define multiple exit plans upfront: Are you selling in five years? Be sure you understand the strategy of your passive investment.

## 6. Tax Efficiency Beyond Deferral

When you use a 1031 exchange, you can postpone paying capital gains tax and something called depreciation recapture. Depreciation recapture is the tax you owe for the extra tax savings you got from claiming depreciation over time.

But there's a bigger question: **Is it always best to avoid taxes forever?**

### Tax Trade-off: Deferral vs. Paying the Tax

- **1031 Exchange + DST**: You fully defer both capital gains and depreciation recapture. You pay zero upfront and just roll into another property. This keeps your investment simple—but can limit growth.

- **1031 Into Private Equity Fund (Passive):** You might pay some or all capital gains and recapture tax but gain access to higher yields (12–17% IRR) and generous depreciation allowances inside the fund.

We'll explore the math behind these options in detail in another chapter.

## 7. Liquidity and Lock-Up Nuances

Liquidity isn't just about money. It's about when and how easily you can access your investment. Different paths—DIY active, 1031 into another property, DST, or private equity fund—each come with their own trade-offs.

### DIY Active Ownership: You're in Control.

If you own the property yourself, you decide when to sell or refinance. Finding a buyer can take time, and costs (like broker fees) may apply. (This would be true for any option).

You can refinance when it makes sense. Lower your rate and/or tap into equity, subject to lender approval and loan terms.

- Pros: Maximum control and flexibility
- Cons: You manage the process—time, stress, effort.

**1031 Exchange into Another Active Property.**

This is active ownership with a twist—you use a 1031 exchange to defer capital gains. You still control the property but must follow IRS rules. We outlined these in chapter one.

You can't access your cash mid-exchange—it must stay tied to the new property.

- Pros: Control + zero immediate tax
- Cons: Strict timelines and locked-up funds during the exchange

**DST and OZ Liquidity: The Lock-In Trap.**

These options are not liquid. DSTs usually have 5-10-year periods; early sales aren't allowed in most cases. OZ require a ten-year hold for the maximum tax benefit and usually cannot refinance mid-project to access equity. Secondary market? Rare. If you sell before the term ends, it's usually at a discount, and you may need sponsor approval (which might involve additional fees).

- Pros: Easy setup, tax deferral, passive
- Cons: Locked up—no control or early access; highest fees and usually lowest returns.

### Private Equity Funds: Balanced Liquidity.

Private equity real estate funds sit between control and convenience. They are like DST in that there isn't liquidity and there usually isn't a secondary market.

- Pros: Usually, higher returns and lower up-front fees than DST
- Cons: No tax shelter like 1031 or DST unless depreciation can be used to offset

### Why Liquidity Matters

- Emergencies happen—health, family, investments.
- Market changes may require quick repositioning.
- Without liquidity, you might be unable to act or pay when it matters.
- You might find an excellent investment opportunity and not have a way to access cash to capitalize on it.

## 8. Sponsor Accountability and Alignment

The passive sponsor (or fund manager) runs everything: buying property, managing it, and selling it. It's vital your interests match theirs, so they work as hard as you do.

### What Does "Sponsor" Mean?

- Sponsor, or General Partner (GP), is the team that sources deals, secures financing, hires property managers, and guides the investment.

- You, the investor, are often a Limited Partner (LP). You provide capital but leave decisions to the sponsor.

### Why Alignment Matters

Sponsors usually earn in two ways:

1. **<u>Fees</u>:** Often 1% one-time for acquisitions and 2–5% annually for managing assets.

2. **<u>Promote or Carried Interest</u>:** A share of profits above a set return (often LPs get 6–10% before the Sponsor gets a profit; this is a "preferred return" for the LP).

Here's why this setup works:

- The Sponsors are paid **only** after you receive your promised return.
- Their incentive is higher performance—earning more only when you earn more.

### Warning Signs of Misalignment

Here's what to watch out for:

- Big upfront fees with little tied to results (more than 3%).
- Weak underwriting—using overly optimistic projections may look good on paper but underperform later.
- Conflicts of interest—when sponsor decisions benefit themselves, not investors. This might include related party deals or pushing more deals to grow assets under management even when it's not best for investors.

### What Good Alignment Looks Like

- Fees are reasonable (in line with industry norms).

- DST, OZ Sponsors: They manage property and distribute income. Some also co-invest, aligning their success with yours. But they often rely heavily on fees, not promotes (profit sharing if the project is successful), which can limit alignment.
- Private Equity Sponsors: Their primary payout comes from the promote structure, after LPs earn their return, aligning success with your success.

## Decision Checklist

Ask sponsors:

- Do they co-invest alongside you?
- What waterfall structure do they use? (Preferred return + promote.)
- Can they show consistent past performance across market cycles?
- Are fees clear and reasonable?
- How do they handle reporting and transparency?
- How do they manage conflicts of interest?

# Closing Thoughts

1. **Active investing costs more than money**—Your time, stress, and risk count.
2. **Passive investing centralizes risk and work**—But pay careful attention to *performance*, *incentives*, and *liquidity*.
3. **DSTs offer simplicity and maximum tax deferral**—But typically limit returns and flexibility.

4. **Private equity + paid-capital model**—By front-loading taxes to unlock higher-yield, professionally managed strategies, you gain superior *after-tax IRR* and control.

5. **1031 exchange remains central**—As a tool to shift smoothly between active, passive, and hybrid investment paths, aligning with your goals and market conditions.

By understanding these eight hidden cost factors, you'll be equipped to make intelligent, flexible investment decisions that grow wealth **AND** preserve your time and peace of mind.

If you would like to see if passive investing in a Fund of Funds is right for you. Go to http://irontoncapital.com/gopassive to choose your best time for your free portfolio review.

Up next: In Chapter 4 we'll dive deep into how to build diversification with four pillars, using these strategies to maximize gains and minimize risk.

# Chapter 4:
# Four Pillars of Diversification

You may have heard about the four pillars of passive real estate investing diversification. We believe that truly effective diversification means more than picking different assets. It means tracking emerging trends and translating them into a workable, updateable strategy that you can adjust as market and needs change. The Four Pillars of Diversification are Geography, Asset Class, Strategy, and Sponsors.

## Pillar 1: Diversify Geography

Of the four pillars, geographic diversification is often the easiest to grasp. Earlier, we were fully invested in Colorado—just in Denver and Colorado Springs. Then in 2023 the Colorado Legislature passed nine new laws that favored tenants and made being a landlord much more difficult.

For example, tenants now have a right of first refusal to renew their lease. If we had a problem tenant—someone paid late, damaged the unit or disturbed neighbors—we could no longer act freely. The tenant now decides if they stay. More bills were passed in 2024, and within a few years, Colorado changed from investor-friendly to investor-hostile. If we had kept all our investments in Colorado, our risk would be much higher, our stress greater and our returns lower.

These kinds of regulatory shifts can happen in any market at any time. By spreading our investments across different geographies, we reduce our exposure to one region's rules.

Traditionally, you'd use a 1031 exchange to swap Colorado real estate for similar property in a high-growth state—deferred taxes allow full reinvestment under the IRS's 3-property/200% rules. These three property replacements can be in different states.

If we had diversified with a 1031 exchange instead of staying locked in Colorado, we could have swapped out our local assets for properties in fast-growing Sunbelt markets—without triggering capital gains taxes.

There are three aspects that can be used to determine where to invest: population growth/change, average home price appreciation, and population migration.

Population growth is a major driver of real-estate markets. Areas where people are moving out—like parts of New York or Illinois—face low demand for homes and apartments, so less pressure on rent and value. By contrast, fast-growing areas need new development. The increase in population means more competition among consumers to buy a home or rent an apartment, which drives rent, appreciation and cashflow growth. (See Figure 4-1.)

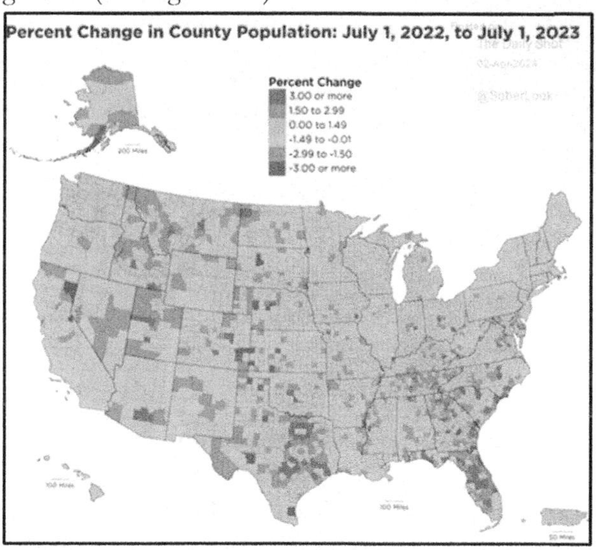


*Map source: Census Bureau.*

**Figure 4-1: Population Change**

But here's the twist: In most comparisons we've run, investors who paid some or all capital gains tax, and reinvested directly into our passive income funds (12–17 % IRR)—while capturing hefty depreciation offsets—outperformed those who took 100 % tax deferral via DSTs yielding 5–6 % cash flow with modest appreciation.

For many of you, finding another active investment to replace your old investment, linked with a 1031 exchange, will be the optimal strategy. In the past, DST was the backup plan. Now private equity funds like Ironton offer another backup for the 1031 investor.

Let's look at the average home price appreciation from 1991-2023 (Figure 4-2).

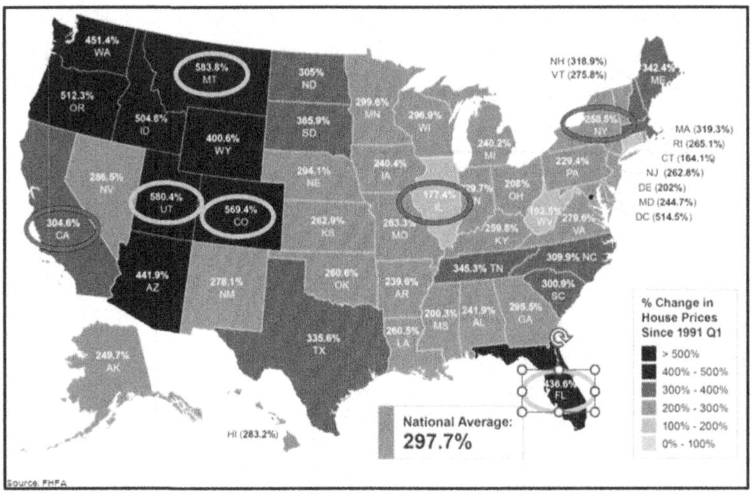


*Map Source: FHFA | Federal Housing Finance Agency*

**Figure 4-2: Average Home Price Appreciation**

States with strong population growth like Utah, Colorado, Arizona, Montana, and Florida all had appreciation that exceeded the US average of 297% from 1991 to 2023.

States with stagnant or declining population, like New York and Illinois, had below average appreciation. California is in the middle; it's growing at a much slower pace. And California's appreciation, as you might expect, is right about at the US average.

The pace of population relocations seems to be accelerating post-COVID. This could be a function of greater acceptance of remote work. (Figure 4-3)

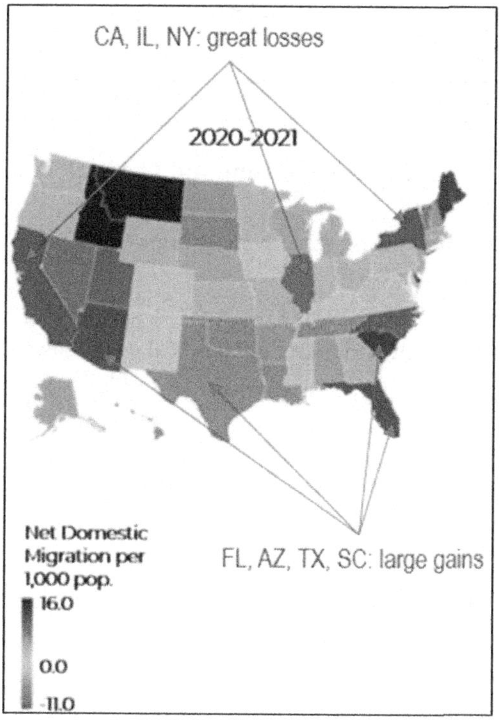


*Source: US Census.*

**Figure 4-3: Population Migration**

Another way to identify population movement is to monitor which states have the most in-bound U-Haul traffic (Figure 4-4).

| State | 2023 Rank | 2022 Rank |
|---|---|---|
| Texas | 1 | 1 |
| Florida | 2 | 2 |
| North Carolina | 3 | 4 |
| South Carolina | 4 | 3 |
| Tennessee | 5 | 6 |
| Idaho | 6 | 10 |
| Washington | 7 | 23 |
| Arizona | 8 | 7 |
| Colorado | 9 | 11 |
| Virginia | 10 | 5 |

*Source: U-Haul.*

**Figure 4-4: Inbound U-Haul Traffic**

These states are among what we consider our 15 top markets.

At Ironton Capital, we focus on Sunbelt states. They show strong population growth and generally fair real estate laws (For example, if a tenant doesn't pay rent, the investor can act).

## Pillar 2: Diversify Asset Class

We believe that diversification across asset classes is equally important. When an investor sells a single-family rental home, a 1031 exchange allows them to reinvest in different kinds of commercial real estate. That action not only defers taxes but also broadens the investor's exposure.

Here are the asset classes:

1. **Residential**
   - Single family homes and condos.

2. **Multifamily**
   - Residential properties other than single-family homes.
     - These include apartment buildings classified as Class A, Class B and Class C, depending on quality and location.
   - Leases typically run for 12 months and require little customization.

3. **Office**
   - These range from single-story suburban buildings to multi-story urban buildings.
   - Most office buildings are developed for multiple tenants; investors generate several revenue streams.
     - This provides income diversity, helping investors to retain cashflow even if a tenant terminates a lease.
   - Compared to other types of commercial real estate properties, office leases tend to be longer: 3-5 years for a "C" building and 5-10 years for an "A" building.
   - In most markets, leases customarily come with built-in annual inflation increases each year.
   - In some markets, the leases are triple net (see next section for an overview of triple net leases).
   - New tenants often demand their space be customized, which is a cost to the landlord (as well as significant project management time).

4. **Industrial**
    - Attractive investment due to their long-term return and leases, as well as low overhead costs.
    - Often "triple-net" (or NNN), where the tenant, not the landlord, is responsible for maintenance, utilities, taxes. This makes management easy—It's the closest thing to "mailbox money."
    - Several types of industrial buildings, which vary in size, layout, format, and typical tenant, provide further opportunities for the investor to diversify.
    - However, rent increases customarily are not as large as other office and multifamily buildings. Lease terms can range from 5-20 years.

5. **Retail**
    - Occupied by businesses (including stores, and restaurants) offering products and services to customers.
    - Amazon and other online stores caused retail foot traffic to decline, but this type of commercial real estate still plays an important role.
    - Like office and industrial, leases are much longer than residential. Inflation increases are usually built in.
    - Like office, retail tenants often expect the landlord to customize their space.

6. **Hotels & Hospitality**
    - Offer both short- and long-term accommodations to travelers, both for leisure and business purposes.
    - Many segments, from economy to luxury, and from very short (nightly) stays to extended stays.

- Higher returns, but higher headaches. You really are managing a business AND a property.

7. **Land**
    - One of the riskiest types of commercial real estate.
    - Historically, it offers the highest return.

8. **Mixed Use**
    - Properties that combine two or more of the above.
    - Many downtown high-rises are considered mixed use.
    - These often have retail on the first few floors and offices, hotels, or apartments above.

9. **Self-Storage**
    - Low cost to operate.
    - Very short lease durations.

Early in our investing career, we concentrated in residential properties. That is typical for new investors. Later, we sold some smaller condos and townhomes and reinvested in commercial properties such as warehouses and office buildings. That change reduced the number of properties we had to track. Even with property managers in place, managing the manager remains work.

We used 1031 exchanges to defer taxes and shift into these commercial assets. The exchange rule allows any real estate, not just similar properties. For example, we could sell multiple rental homes and exchange them into a warehouse.

Another option when selling is to use a 1031 exchange with a DST or OZ as a replacement. This achieves a pure passive investment. Typically returns are 5–6% cash yield with 2–3% appreciation—but usually lag what an active strategy could yield.

A third option is to pay some or all the capital gains tax and invest in private equity focused on real estate. This achieves the goal of moving from active to passive and can generate much higher returns than the DST. Some private equity investments also offer accelerated depreciation in the first year to offset some/all your capital gain. Net, this often yields stronger after-tax returns than deferring everything into a DST.

Office buildings in Denver were a good investment before COVID in 2020. Post-COVID, most office buildings are experiencing increased vacancy rates, and higher concessions to attract tenants. Medical offices are a notable exception. If you have all your money tied up in one asset class, an event like COVID can really change your outlook.

In our personal portfolio we now hold about 65% in residential and multifamily properties. These asset classes historically offer lower returns compared to other commercial types. The upside is they also tend to be less volatile—during economic downturns they perform more reliably.

Some sub-sectors do even better in a recession than in a growing economy. These are called counter-cyclical. For example, many apartment renters will need to trade down in the amount of space they can afford, or move in with a roommate, during a recession. As a result, self-storage often has an uptick in demand in a recession.

More luxurious hospitality offerings perform well in an economic expansion but are among the first of the corporate and personal spending items that get cut back in a recession. The economy segment of hospitality often takes share from the more expensive hotels in a recession.

This is why it's not enough to simply choose a couple of set asset classes for diversification and stay there. To truly manage your risk, you must keep your finger on the pulse of the market and be ready to shift into emerging assets as their time comes. This is why we have monthly live updates on the state of the market so you can be in position as the market trends change.

As our gift to you to help you on your investing journey, go to https://irontoncapital.com/marketupdates to get invited to our next live update.

## Pillar 3: Diversify Strategy

We also believe that diversification across investment strategy is essential. There are three broad strategies real-estate investors use:

- **Buy and Hold** (also called "Income") – Acquiring a property in good condition, managing it for steady rental income.

- **Value-Add** (also called "**Improvement**") – Purchasing a property needing repairs or better management, then improving it to raise value and income.

- **Development** (also called "New Build") – Building a property from raw land or redeveloping a site into something new.

Your personal risk tolerance will help determine which strategy or combination of strategies you choose. Risk tolerance represents how much change or uncertainty you can live comfortably within your investments. For example, younger investors may accept higher risk for higher potential returns; investors closer to retirement often favor more stable, lower risk choices.

- Higher risk often means higher return.
- Lower risk generally means lower return.

Investors that have accumulated enough to meet their financial goals usually pick lower risk, lower return choices. Investors that are still building their wealth are often more receptive to higher risk, higher return options.

## Buy and Hold

When people first think of real estate investment, this is the strategy they hear about. Buy and Hold properties are properties in great condition, being managed well, and providing a reliable cashflow. They may or may not be in a great location.

These are often newer properties, or older properties that have just come off a significant renovation program and are in great shape. You can purchase a property like this easily on your own.

A more practical—and tax advantageous—method is to purchase some shares in a REIT (Real Estate Investment Trust). This enables you to get a diversified portfolio of many properties (usually all in the buy and hold strategy, and in one asset class, but in many locations). REITs have a tax advantage for many people, in that their income is usually taxed at a lower rate than your marginal income tax rate, especially if you are in a higher tax bracket. (Ask your CPA for additional information.)

Another great thing about REITs is that many of them are publicly traded (like the stock market), so you can buy and sell (e.g., have access to liquidity) on a much more flexible basis than if you own the underlying assets directly.

A downside to REITs is that they are not allowed to pass through depreciation (a passive tax write-off for many investors) to their owners. Directly owning real estate allows you to get access to that depreciation.

Finally, non-recourse loans are often available for REITs and large (over $5 MM) multifamily loans. This means you may not have to personally guarantee the loan if something goes wrong or the market changes. While this type of financing has a lot of pros and cons, many larger investors value non-recourse loans. Lenders for smaller investments almost always require personal guarantees.

### Advantages of Buy and Hold

- Often cashflows right away.
- Generally, the lowest risk of the real estate strategies.
- Most predictable cashflow.
- Easiest to finance, and usually on great terms (relative to other asset classes).
- Frequently, non-recourse lending is an option if loan size is large; else personal guarantee will be likely needed.
- Usually, easier to sell.
- Smallest need for special expertise to do well.
- May offer depreciation tax write-offs if you invest directly.
- Often, pride of ownership.
- If in a REIT, you can buy and sell easily, almost like trading stocks.

### Disadvantages of Buy and Hold

- Most expensive to purchase.
- Lowest return on investment.
- May not offer depreciation tax write-off if via a REIT.
- Often, least upside for above-average appreciation.

<u>1031 Pathway:</u> Defer gains by swapping rental assets into similar or more passive properties (e.g., triple-net office or industrial).

Alternative: Sell and pay some/all capital gains to invest in a passive private equity fund, delivering steady yield with depreciation benefits. Though taxable, the overall after-tax IRR (12–17%) often outperforms a multi-year, lower-yield 1031+DST roll-up.

**Bottom Line: Safer, less work, and less return.**

## Value-Add

Value-Add properties are those which are not in great condition. Any property, without constant care and thoughtful oversight, will eventually devolve from a pristine Buy and Hold to a Value-Add project. This might be in condition of the units themselves, the common areas, or both. They may also have poor management and/or deferred maintenance in the infrastructure (e.g., elevators, HVAC systems).

A common way this happens is when an active investor buys a property and has the energy to keep it in top quality condition. As they age, health problems interfere with their ability to take care of the investment. Their spouse and/or kids usually lack the passion and expertise to provide the right oversight to the property manager. Since by this point their mortgage is either paid off, or has a minimal payment, there is no urgency to maximize the cashflow.

There is a strong incentive to pass property to your heirs. If the older owner dies, their kids will inherit the property (assuming the estate plan is set up this way). If they purchased it for $1 million thirty years ago, it might be worth $5 million today. If they sold it while they were alive, they would owe tax on a $4 million capital gain (plus depreciation recapture, which we will discuss in a later chapter).

If their kids inherit it, usually they will be able to get an appraisal for the value at the time of their death. That becomes their tax basis in the property. So, their starting point is now $5 million. They can sell the next day for $5 million, and no capital gains (or depreciation recapture) are due. This is the among the best ways to transfer wealth between generations.

All the while, the property has degraded, has more deferred maintenance, and usually low occupancy and below-market rents. The kids often sell the property ASAP after the probate process is wrapped up. Unsurprisingly, these properties will often trade at a significant discount to what a similar Buy and Hold property in better condition will sell for. Not all Value-Add properties follow this path, but many do.

One additional attractive dimension of Value-Add projects is the depreciation. You can think of depreciation as an interest-free loan from the IRS. For a residential property, you can "depreciate" it over 27.5 years. (Figure 4-5)

| | |
|---:|---:|
| Initial Value | $4,000,000 |
| Land | $1,250,000 |
| Improvements | $2,750,000 |
| Years | 27.50 |
| Depreciation / Year | $100,000 |

**Figure 4-5: Depreciation Example**

Your CPA can help you split up the value of your purchase between the land and the improvements (e.g., the building). In this example, you would write off $100,000 per year.

From the IRS point of view, it is as if you wrote a check to some vendor for that amount, and it reduces your income (and tax bill) that year. Since you don't actually write this check, you get to keep the cash without the tax. When you sell the property, you must true up with the IRS (which is called "depreciation recapture"). For an older property, you can often accelerate the depreciation to generate even larger write-offs in the first year or two. This is covered in more detail later in this book.

## Advantages of Value-Add Projects

- Much less expensive to purchase.
- Much higher potential return on investment if you know what you are doing or hire an experienced team.
- Potentially larger depreciation tax write-offs in years one and two.

## Disadvantages of Value-Add Projects

- Limited, or negative, cashflow to start.
- A significant renovation budget is usually needed.
- Usually requires a construction loan vs. more favorable long-term financing.
- Recourse financing is almost always required.
- Project management and turn-around property management specialists required.
- Much easier to make a costly mistake than the Buy and Hold strategy.

1031 Pathway: Exchange a Buy and Hold asset into a Value-Add project, redeploying full proceeds to enhance tax-deferred returns.

Alternative: Sell and invest in our private equity fund with Value-Add strategies that include property upgrades, operational improvements, and instant depreciation deductions, which are more efficient than tying up capital in a single, active project. Returns are typically higher and are risk diversified across multiple assets.

**Bottom Line: More work, more risk, and (potentially) much higher returns.**

## Development

Finally, Development projects refer to building a property from scratch. You would first need to do a demand study to be sure your project would be right for the location.

For example, if you wanted to build a new economy extended-stay hotel, you'd do a study to determine:

- Current demand for lodging in that market
- How that demand was disaggregated across different segments (extended stay vs. 1-2 nights, economy vs. luxury, submarket, etc.)
- Projected market growth

In this example, you'd love to see that 18% of the stays in the market are over seven nights (e.g., extended stay), but that only 10% of thc available hotel beds in the market are configured as extended stay hotels (e.g., the rooms have mini-kitchens, on-site laundry and other amenities for longer term guests). There's a lot more to a demand analysis, but this illustrates it at a high level.

Once you know there is demand for what you want to build, you'd look for land that would be appropriate to serve that need. The starting point could be one of the following.

### Raw Land

- Cheapest to purchase.
- May or may not have the correct zoning in place.
- May involve a lengthy process with local government planning authority to get permits (to build).

- Often the longest project, with highest risk, and on average, highest returns.
- You typically won't generate income while holding it, so you need to have enough reserves to cover bank interest payments, and pay property taxes, insurance, and architects while you go through the permitting process.

### Improved Land

- Intermediate cost of the three development options.
- Already zoned correctly.
- May have some/all the pre-construction design and engineering complete.
- In some cases, projects are sold "shovel ready" where you can pull the permit and start right away.
- Fewer surprises: Lower risk, faster timelines, and lower returns than raw land.
- Fewer holding costs before construction.

### Existing Site

- Demolish ("scrape") an existing building and replace it with something new (usually a lot bigger).
- Often zoned correctly but might require some of the re-zoning steps in "raw land".
- Often, existing buildings generate cashflow to offset holding costs while you navigate government paperwork.

If you are highly confident that you'll (eventually) get your government approvals, you can work on the other development tasks in parallel to save time.

Some sample tasks would include:

- Environmental reviews
- Soil testing and civil engineering (to design the foundation)
- Architectural and engineering design for the building
- Sharing these reports with general contractors to get bids
- Meeting with banks to explain the project, assess interest, and gather term sheets

Once you have your permits (i.e., you are "shovel ready"), you can close on the loan with the bank and get started. Either you will need to be on site frequently to assess progress, quality check, and solve the innumerable problems that come up, or have an "owners rep" that does all of this for you.

We are continually amazed at how many people have an interest in becoming a real estate developer. It sounds alluring to people, for some reason, but it really is a lot of work. There is a big satisfaction at the end when you see the finished product (especially if you manage to make a profit in the process).

## Advantages of Development

- Very high potential return on investment if you know what you are doing and/or hire an experienced team.
- Most problem-solving and potential for creative solutions if that's what you enjoy.

## Disadvantages of Development

- Limited, or negative, cashflow to start.
- Always requires a construction loan vs. more favorable long-term financing.
- Recourse financing is almost always required.
- Advanced project management and construction specialists are essential.
- No depreciation in early years for passive losses.
- Not recommended if you can't handle stress.
- Has the most problem solving if you are NOT into that.

1031 Pathway: Exchange a Buy and Hold asset into a Development project, redeploying full proceeds to enhance tax-deferred returns.

Alternative: Sell and invest in our private equity fund with Development strategy. Returns are often higher (even after tax), than tying up capital in a single, active project or a DST, and are risk diversified across multiple assets and geographies.

**Bottom Line: The highest effort, highest risk, and highest returns.**

There are as many ways to build a real estate portfolio as there are ways to build a stock portfolio.

You can exchange from a stable Buy and Hold into a high-growth Value-Add or even launch a Development project, all without triggering immediate capital gains—so your capital compound continues uninterrupted. (We are personally not interested in Buy and Hold since we have the experience to pursue the two more advanced strategies that generate much high returns in most economic environments. However, everyone will have a different perspective on this.)

A successful real estate portfolio isn't just diverse in property type—it's diverse in strategy. 1031 exchanges allow you to navigate between rental, renovation, and development strategies—on your terms, depending on your view of the market cycle — while keeping your gains working for you instead of paying taxes.

## Pillar 4: Diversify Sponsors

Finally, we believe that sponsor diversification is a critical but often overlooked pillar. In real estate investing, the sponsor (or general partner) is the entity that selects, acquires, manages and disposes of the property. If you make multiple investments with the same sponsor, your portfolio may be exposed to that sponsor's weaknesses.

A smart use of a 1031 exchange lets you spread proceeds across different sponsors or funds in one transaction. Whether you invest in multifamily, industrial, self-storage, retail or hospitality, you benefit by varying the sponsors you partner with.

For example, we once invested with one GP (general partner) who subcontracted property management (PM). The PM was capable but had no experience in that specific asset type. The GP assumed conversion would be seamless. The result? The PM under-performed. The GP had to replace them mid-project, creating distraction and delay. Because we had been entirely with that sponsor, our full investment was affected.

Had we diversified across sponsors, we could have avoided putting "all our eggs in one basket" and reduced the impact of that single misstep.

Ideally, you build a portfolio across many sponsors. Each sponsor has unique strengths, blind spots and areas of specialization—by investing across several sponsors, you limit the overlap of risk.

## Closing Thoughts

It's important to be mindful of creating a balanced portfolio across all 4 Pillars of Diversification. This is what can enable you to generate strong returns in the 17-20% annual range while having a well-managed level of risk.

By combining 1031 exchange flexibility with multi-sponsor investments, you build resilience—not just in geography and asset class, but in leadership. You gain the assurance that even if one sponsor falters, your overall strategy stays intact.

By combining sponsor diversification through 1031 exchange flexibility with selective private fund investment, you gain:

- Resilience—Diverse sponsor expertise shields against singular missteps.
- High returns—Funds structured for yield and value creation.
- Tax efficiency—Depreciation continues to work against recognized capital gains.

Our Investor Relations team has set aside some time for you if you would like to see if passive investing is right for you. Go to http://irontoncapital.com/gopassive to choose your best time for your free portfolio review.

# Chapter 5: DST in Depth

Delaware Statutory Trusts (DSTs) are an increasingly popular choice for passive real estate, especially in 1031 exchanges. (According to an Exchange Trends Report, DST allocations from 1031 exchange sellers nearly doubled from 2023 to early 2025.) In this chapter, we'll dig deeper into how DSTs work, their strengths and weaknesses, questions to ask, a simple return case study, and common mistakes to avoid. **Be sure to look at Chapter 8 for a ten-year cash flow model comparison of DST** to the other common passive investment strategies vs. Do Nothing (keep your active rental) vs. a 1031 exchange!

## DST Structure and Strategy

### How DSTs Work

A DST is an investment vehicle where multiple investors own fractional interests in institutional-quality real estate—but without day-to-day management. Professional sponsors handle leasing, maintenance, and eventual sale.

For those familiar, DSTs are analogous to Real Estate Investment Trusts (REITs). One critical difference is that shares in a REIT are **not** eligible to participate in a 1031 exchange.

DSTs qualify for 1031 exchanges because of IRS Revenue Ruling 2004-86: they meet the "like-kind" requirement of real estate ownership. There are strict rules—"the seven deadly sins"—which limit what sponsors can do after buying a property.

We won't dive into the seven rules here, but the net effect is DSTs must make relatively low-risk, low/no value-add investments. You can expect lower risk and lower overall returns as a result. Higher risk/return strategies like new development or value-add projects <u>do not work</u> with the DST laws.

### Investment Mechanics

- Minimum Investment: Often $100,000 or higher.
- Hold Period: Typically, 5–10 years until the property sells.
- Income: Investors receive monthly or quarterly rent distributions.
- Tax Benefits:
  - **Depreciation**: A cost deducted from taxable rental income over time.
  - **Cost Segregation:** (Rare in DSTs) accelerates deductions early.
  - **1031 Deferral**: No capital gains taxes until exit.
- Debt Structures: Many DSTs use non-recourse debt, shielding investors personally in case of problems. Some are debt-free, offering stronger cash flow and lower risk. The tradeoff is that the IRR is lower.

## Pros and Cons

### Pros:

- Passive Investment: No management duties—tenants and toilets are handled by others.
- Access to Premium Assets: You can invest in large, well-maintained properties (retail, multifamily, industrial, medical) otherwise out of reach for an individual investor.
- Diversify Easily: Small investments can spread across multiple assets or markets. A luxury for investors.
- Stable Income: Many DST properties offer long-term, triple-net leases, providing a higher degree of rental certainty.

- **Non-Recourse Loans**: These loans limit your liability to just your DST share, not your personal assets.
- **Streamlined Process**: Deals are pre-vetted with financing, leases, and PPMs (Private Placement Memorandums). You still need to do your own due diligence.

**Cons:**

- **Lack of Control**: You can't veto decisions or participate in management.
- **Illiquidity**: It is extremely difficult to successfully exit before the DST sells the property. The secondary market for DST is extremely limited and illiquid and specialized. The most likely buyers are other investors in the same DST, and even then, you usually see the exiting investor face a steep haircut on the trade.
- **Fees**: Sponsors charge acquisition and asset management fees that lower returns.
- **Sponsor Risk**: Returns depend heavily on the sponsor's experience and integrity.
- **Leverage Risk**: High debt increases earnings—but also elevates risks if rates rise or tenants default. This is usually less of a problem with DST, since most are conservative with debt.
- **Single-Asset Risk**: Returns depend entirely on one property—if leases end or markets decline, income drops. Of course, many DSTs invest in multiple assets to offset this risk factor.
- **Accredited Investor Only**: Typically, available only to investors who meet SEC requirements (net worth greater than $1M or income greater than $200K).

## Due Diligence Checklist

There are eight factors we recommend reviewing with your financial team when planning your investments We'll cover these in Chapter 11.

## Case Study: Net Returns After Expenses

### Scenario

- **Investment:** $200,000 DST investment in a medical office building
- **Hold Period:** 8 years
- **Cash Flow**: 6% cash-on-cash → $12,000/year × 8 = $96,000.
- **Appreciation**: Property sale generates 4% annual growth → ~$66,000 gain.
- **Fees**: Initial 2%, annual asset fee 1% → ~$36,000 total.
- **Net Returns**:
  - Gross income: $162,000
  - Fees: -$36,000
  - Net: $126,000 over 8 years = ~4.5% annual net return
- **Tax Savings**: Depreciation shelters income each year and defers gains. With 1031 exchange on exit, taxes are delayed until a future sale.

This example shows clear income and tax benefits—but emphasizes the need to understand fees, leverage, and sponsor quality.

## Diversification Approach

We explored the Four Pillars of Diversification in Chapter 4. Here's how DSTs implement diversification.

- **Geography**: Can be excellent. Many DSTs invest all over the country or offer regional specialization.
- **Asset Class:** Often excellent. Many DSTs focus on a particular investment class, such as only retail or only industrial. You can invest in multiple DSTs to get the exposure you want.
- **Strategy**: Almost exclusively Buy and Hold; it's impractical to invest in Value Add or Development due to IRS limitations. This means the DST usually has lower risk and lower return than other passive alternatives. For investors in wealth protection mode, this is often a great alignment. For investors still in wealth building mode, DSTs might not be the best option.
- **Sponsor:** The Sponsor's expertise and track record always matters, but our opinion is that it matters the most for the higher risk / higher reward strategies. For DST, being focused on Buy and Hold, it matters a little less. Many DST operators have massive scale and deep expertise (be sure to double check!).

## Common Pitfalls and Mistakes

- **Not Vetting the Sponsor**: Poor sponsors can mismanage, increasing vacancy or missing payments.
- **Ignoring Debt Risk**: High leverage or variable interest can hurt income if rents drop or rates spike.
- **Buying Blind**: Assuming any DST is solid—property details matter more than structure.

- **Dependent on Single Tenant**: If one tenant fails in a single-asset DST, the whole investment suffers.
- **Overconcentration**: Investing too much in one DST increases risk.
- **Expecting Quick Liquidity**: DSTs are illiquid; early exit is unlikely.
- **Not Seeking Professional Help**: You should consult legal, tax, and financial advisers.

## Closing Thoughts

DSTs offer a hands-off path into good real estate with tax deferral. They can suit investors seeking passive income without landlord duties. But they carry limitations: lack of control, illiquidity, debt risk, and sponsor dependency. Thorough due diligence is vital—evaluate sponsors, structures, properties, and markets carefully. In the later chapters, we'll compare DSTs to the other passive alternatives and show where each fits best.

# Chapter 6: Private Placements (Syndications) and Fund of Funds

Private Placements (PP) (often referred to as "Syndications") and Fund of Funds (FOF) are another path for passive real estate investing. Unlike DSTs, these involve actively managed strategies and offer higher return potential—at the tradeoff of complexity and risk.

**Be sure to look at Chapter 8 for a ten-year cash flow model comparison** of Private Placements/Syndications to the other common passive investment strategies vs. Do Nothing (keep your active rental) vs. a 1031 exchange!

## Private Placements (PP)

**Private Placement (or Syndication)** is a single real estate deal offered directly to a group of investors. It might be one apartment building or a multi-tenant property, often sponsored by a trusted manager. No diversification happens in the investment, so it's up to you, the investor, to choose a diversified portfolio.

## Fund of Funds (FOF)

A **Fund of Funds**, like Ironton Capital, pools money from many investors to buy several properties under one strategy. For example, a fund might focus on multifamily communities in fast-growing suburbs. The goal is to maximize diversification.

### How They Work

- Usually only accredited investors can participate—at least $1 million net worth or significant income (single households over $200K, dual households over $300K).
- You contribute capital (minimum from $50K to $250K+).
- The General Partner (GP) or "Sponsor" uses that capital to buy, manage, and sell properties.
- You receive cash flow from rent and a share of profits at exit.
- GP fees include annual management fees (often 1–2%) and a "carry" (a portion of profits, typically around 20%). The carry often increases for highly successful projects.

### Why They Matter

- Professional management gives access to institutional-quality deals you couldn't get alone. Many institutional deals require a $1 million+ minimum investment.
- Tax benefits like depreciation and cost segregation help reduce taxable income quickly for some funds.
- Diversification across multiple properties, markets, and asset types helps spread risk.

## Pros and Cons

### Pros:

- **Higher Returns**: Targets range from 8% up to 20% IRR after fees and expenses, depending on fund type and strategy.
- **Tax Shields**: Methods like cost segregation reduce taxable income in early years.

- **Diversification**: Spread risk across several properties and regions.
- **Active Management**: Sponsors can improve and reposition properties to add value.

**Cons:**

- **Long Lock-Up**: Money is tied up for 4–6 years (sometimes as long as 10).
- **High Fees**: Management fees plus performance share reduces returns.
- **Less Control**: You rely on the GP's skill and decisions.
- **Riskier Assets**: New development, value-add and opportunistic deals face bigger market and lease risks vs. Buy and Hold deals.
- **Illiquidity**: Hard or impossible to exit early—no public market.
- **Accreditation Required**: Not open to regular investors due to SEC rules.
- **Limited 1031 Exchange:** Generally, it is not possible (unless there is a TIC). However, accelerated depreciation can offset your capital gains from the sale to give many of the same tax benefits.

# How TIC Fits In

Tenancy in Common (TIC) is another form of shared property ownership, different from PP/FOF.

- With TIC, you own an actual portion of a single property—often with voting rights and legal shared ownership.
- Some private placements are structured as TIC deals—giving partial control and tax parity.

- These can offer more control than PP/FOF but add legal complexity, fees, and require consensus among co-owners.
- Sometimes you can use a 1031 exchange with a TIC. (Other structures potentially exist for sponsors accepting 1031 capital, but they are niche and rare.)
- A TIC allows for 1031 exchange into a PP. However, most Sponsors don't allow it, since it adds complexity and cost. It might make sense for larger (over $1 million) investments so that the significant legal costs make sense in the overall context.

## Diversification Approach: Private Placements and Syndications

We explored the Four Pillars of Diversification in Chapter 4. Here's how PPs implement diversification.

- **Geography**: Usually focused on one city.
- **Asset Class:** Usually focused on one asset class.
- **Strategy**: Usually focused on one strategy. While Buy and Hold is certainly possible in a Syndication, many will select Value Add or Development for great returns (at the tradeoff of higher risk).
- **Sponsor:** Usually a single sponsor.

If you have a diverse portfolio of real estate investments, you might not need additional diversification in your next investment. If so, a Syndication could be a great fit for you. If you have a limited number of real estate investments, this degree of concentration might not be in your best interest.

## Diversification Approach: Fund of Funds (FOF)

Here's how FOFs implement diversification.

- **Geography**: Often multiple cities and states.
- **Asset Class:** Some funds will specialize in a single class; others will incorporate a broader set of asset classes to further spread risk.
- **Strategy**: Some funds will specialize in a single strategy; others will incorporate a broader set of strategies to further spread risk. While Buy and Hold is certainly possible in a FOF or PP, many will select Value Add or Development for great returns (at the tradeoff of higher risk). Spreading the portfolio across multiple investments reduces the risk.
- **Sponsor:** Some funds will specialize in one Sponsor; others will seek multiple Sponsors as another way to diversify risk.

If your wealth is at the right amount for your family goals, wealth preservation is likely your goal. FOF and Syndications are likely too high risk/reward for you. If you are focused on wealth building, FOF and syndications are likely an appropriate tool for your family.

## Case Study: Net Returns After Expenses

### Scenario

- **Investment**: $500,000 in a value-add opportunity fund.
- **Hold Period**: 7 years.
- **Strategy**: Buy older retail center, renovate, re-lease, then sell.

**Financials**

- **Target IRR**: 15% (income + growth).
- **Fees**: 1.5% annual management + 20% carried interest.
- **Tax Benefits**: $30,000/yr depreciation (cost segregation).

**Net Results (Simplified)**

- **Gross Return**: ~$1.2 million at exit.
- **Fees Paid**: ~$200,000 over 7 years.
- **Tax Benefit**: ~$210,000 in early depreciation.
- **Net Gain**: ~+$710,000 over 7 years ≈ 14% net IRR.

This case shows that, despite fees and lock-up, the fund can produce strong after-tax returns—if the strategy works as planned.

## Closing Thoughts

Private placements and fund of funds offer a powerful way to invest in real estate with professional management, higher return targets, and tax advantages. But they also come with complexity, fees, long timelines, and risk. Choose your time at irontoncapital.com/gopassive to see if FOF my be right for you.

To benefit from this route, you need to:

- Pick sponsors with proven track records.
- Understand the fee and management structure.
- Match the investment's goals to your wealth plan and risk tolerance.
- Perform rigorous due diligence using structured checklists (see Chapter 11).

# Chapter 7:
# OZ Opportunity Zones and July 2025 Tax Law

Opportunity Zone Funds (OZ) offer a powerful way for investors to defer or reduce capital gains taxes by investing in businesses or property in designated low-income areas. Since the program was created in 2017, it has attracted $85 billion in investment according to the Wall Street Journal.

The program evolved significantly. The One Big Beautiful Bill Act of July 2025 made major updates—making the program permanent, easier to use, and perhaps more transparent.

Before we dive in, understand this critical point: **Investing in a Qualified Opportunity Fund is required to receive OZ tax benefits**. Simply buying property located in an OZ outside of a Fund structure yields no advantage. NOTE: In this chapter, we'll refer to "Phase I" as the rules before the July 2025 tax bill, and "Phase II" as the new rules.

**Be sure to look at Chapter 8 for a ten-year cash flow model comparison** of OZ investing versus the other common passive investment strategies, versus keeping your active rental (Do Nothing), versus completing a 1031 exchange.

Appendix C offers a brief review of the recent tax law changes. The OZ strategy changed most of the six passive strategies, which follow.

## OZ Structure and Strategy

- Opportunity Zones (OZs) are specific census tracts deemed "low-income"—intended to boost development through tax incentives to eligible investors.
- Investors must place recognized capital gains into a Qualified Opportunity Fund (QOF), which then invests in OZ property or businesses (QOZBs).

**IMPORTANT NOTE** Be sure to check the OZ Phase I zip codes and census tracts closely. (OZs are census-tract based, not city-wide.) Many of the original investment areas are far from what most people would consider "low income". For example, in Denver, most of the city of Englewood is in an OZ.

Here's a view of Colorado's initial OZ-qualified areas (Figure 7-1).

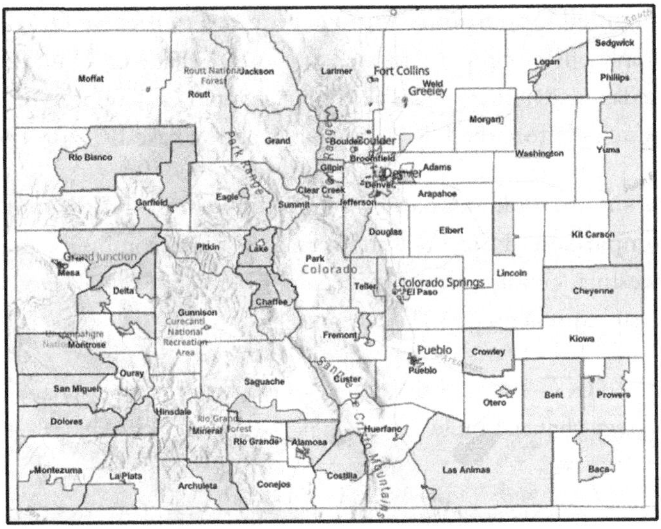


Source: https://oedit.colorado.gov/colorado-opportunity-zone-program

**Figure 7-1: Initial OZ-Qualified Zones**

Let's zoom into Denver metro (Figure 7-2):

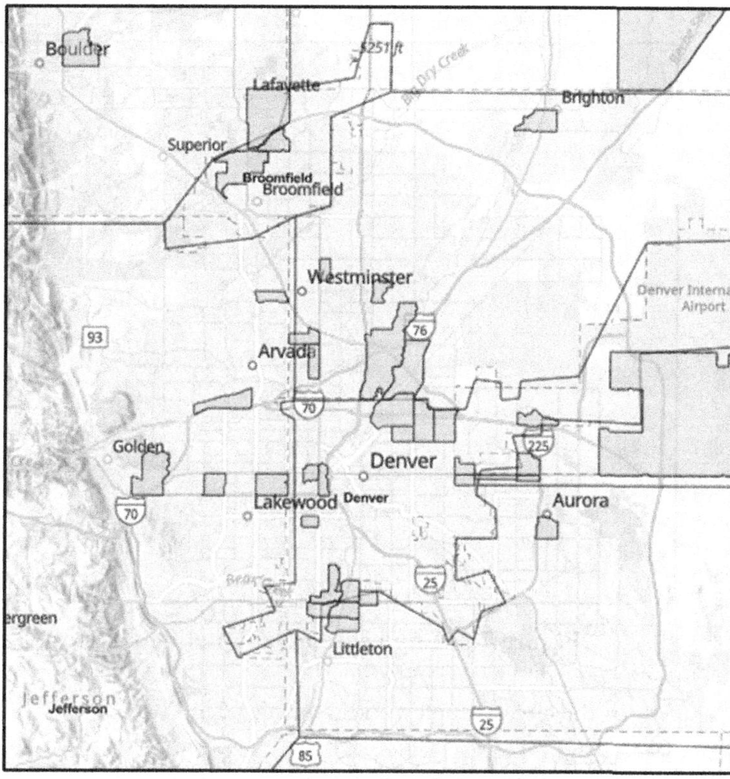


**Figure 7-2: Denver Metro OZ-Qualified Zones**

You can see some parts of affluent Boulder and central Denver were included!

If we zoom in to Englewood, the first city south of the City of Denver (Figure 7-3)…

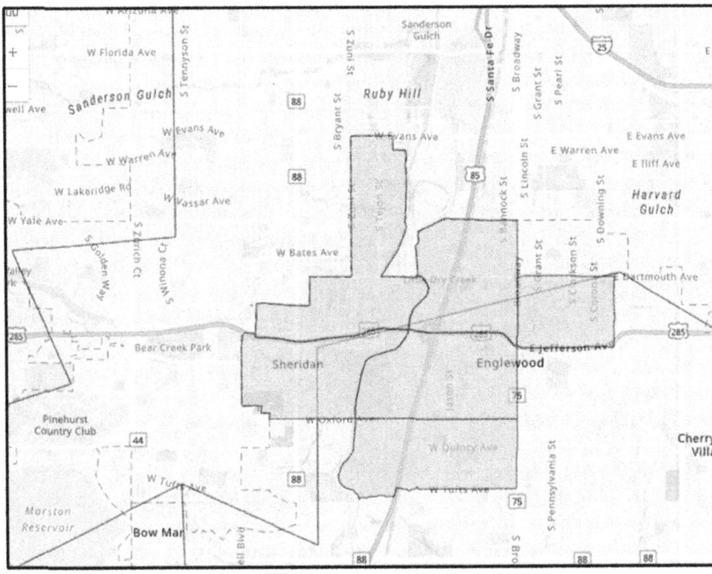


**Figure 7-3: Englewood OZ-Qualified Zones**

…most of the city of Englewood was an OZ in Phase I!

Figure 7-4 is a demographic snapshot of one Englewood census tract as illustration.

| Metric | Englewood, CO | U.S. Average | Comparison |
|---|---|---|---|
| **Median Household Income** | $82,016 (2023) | ~$69,700 (approx.) | ~18% above |
| **Average Household Income** | ~$109,081 | (Higher than median; U.S. ~ $100k) | Robust local earning power |
| **Per Capita Income** | ~$53,400–$59,529 | ~$36,000 | Significantly higher |
| **Percent with Bachelor's+** | **~46%** | **~35%** | Well-educated community |
| **Poverty Rate** | **8.10%** | **12.40%** | Lower poverty level |
| **Home Value (Median)** | 530,000 | 300,000 | Higher home equity |

**Figure 7-4: Englewood Census Tract**

You can see in this example that Englewood is not rural and far from an economically disadvantaged area. This attractive market made a great choice for an OZ investment in Phase I of the program, which ends in 2026. There are examples all over the US like this. In Phase I of OZ, governors got to pick census tracts meeting certain criteria, and investors got tax benefits for putting money there.

According to the Wall Street Journal, GOP lawmakers, largely happy with the OZ program, aimed to address perceived weaknesses. They eliminated the governors' ability to pick tracts contiguous to low-income areas, which could prevent egregious examples in better-off neighborhoods, such as the Englewood example above.

The new version of the tax bill likely won't permit urban areas like Englewood. The tradeoff is the tax benefits in many ways have been improved. Rural spaces in OZ Phase I didn't get much—just 8.5% of overall investment, according to the congressional Joint Committee on Taxation.

According to WSJ analysis, even with bigger tax breaks, attracting rural investment might prove difficult. Counties far from major highways aren't always great fits for distribution centers or factories. They don't work well for real-estate developers' standard fare of multifamily-housing projects. And they often lack the utility access necessary for industrial projects.

## OZ Clock Cheat Sheet: Timelines

- **180-Day Reinvestment Window**: You must invest eligible capital gains into a QOF within 180 days of realizing the gain.
- **Pass-Through Entity Clock**: For gains from partnerships, S-corps, or similar entities, the 180-day clock typically starts when the entity realizes the gain, unless you elect otherwise.

- **10-Year Hold for Exclusion**: Hold your QOF interest for at least 10 years to qualify for the permanent exclusion of appreciation on the QOF investment itself.
- **Inclusion Events**: Selling your QOF interest, gifting it, or otherwise disposing of it before 2026 accelerates the recognition of your deferred gain.

**Important**: The character of your original gain (short-term vs. long-term capital gain) is preserved through the deferral.

## How OZ Phase I Worked Before July 2025

- **Deferral**: Capital gains tax was postponed until December 31, 2026, or until you sold the investment—whichever came first.
- **Step-Up in Basis**:
  - 10% increase after 5 years
  - 5% additional after 7 years
- **Tax-Free Growth**: If held for 10+ years, any increase in value was completely tax-free.

## Example from Original OZ Structure:

Mike sold investment property generating a $1 million capital gain. He invested that $1 million into a QOF within 180 days.

- **Year 5**: His basis increased 10%, so his taxable gain dropped from $1M to $900K.
- **Year 7**: Basis increased another 5% (15% total), reducing taxable gain to $850K.
- **December 31, 2026**: Mike recognized and paid tax on the $850K deferred gain.

- **Year 10+**: His QOF investment grew to $3 million. Because he held for 10+ years, he could elect to exclude the $2 million appreciation from taxation. He paid tax only on the original $850K (which he had already paid by 12/31/2026), making the $2 million gain completely tax-free.

## What Changed in the 2025 Law

The July 2025 law made several key updates:

- **Program is permanent**; no more end-date in 2026. However, deferral on originally invested gains still ends on December 31, 2026, for investments made in prior years.
- **Rolling, 10-year zone designations** begin in 2026. States select OZ census tracts every decade, effective Jan 1 of the following year.
- **New timeline**:
    - Deferral lasts until 5 years after your investment or until sale, whichever comes first.
    - After 5 years, you keep 10% of your original gains tax-free.
    - The 7-year extra basis bonus is eliminated—except for rural OZ funds, which receive a 30% step-up at 5 years.
    - You still pay no tax on fund growth after 10 years, up to 30 years.
- **Stricter rules on zone selection**: Next round limits OZs to tracts with median incomes ≤ 70% of the metro median or high poverty levels. "Contiguous" tracts and blanket zones, like Puerto Rico's, are no longer allowed.
- **New reporting requirements**: QOFs, QOZBs, and investors must report details such as census tract locations, jobs created, and

investor identities. Fines for non-compliance can reach $50,000 per return.

- **Rural Opportunity Funds (QROFs)**: Special OZs investing in rural areas get better benefits:
    - 30% basis step-up after 5 years
    - Lower cost for upgrades to existing buildings (50% vs. 100%).

## Tax Timing and Strategy Tips

- **Final Chance Under Old Rules**: Investments made before Dec 31, 2026, claim 5% and 7% step-ups. Starting Jan 1, 2027, only 10% applies, with rural QROFs eligible for 30%.
- **"Dead Zone" Risk**: Some investors may delay during 2026–27 waiting for new rules, but this may slow new capital in designated areas.
- **New Zones to Watch**: All states can pick new tracts in 2026; Puerto Rico loses blanket coverage(per Brookings).

## What Didn't Change

- You still must invest **capital gains only**—ordinary income may not be invested.
- **No fund-of-funds** allowed—smaller investors can't enter through intermediary funds.
- **No special programs for affordable housing** beyond existing availability.

## Pros and Cons

### Pros:

- **Extraordinary Tax Benefits**: OZs offer a rare combination: deferral of capital gains, partial forgiveness after 5 years (10%, or 30% for rural OZs), and complete tax exemption on appreciation after 10 years. (Particularly attractive after taxable sales when 1031 exchange was not possible or optimal.)
- **Social Impact**: Investors can support underdeveloped communities and potentially create jobs or improve local infrastructure while earning returns.
- **Permanent and Predictable**: The 2025 law removed the sunset date, giving OZs a long-term horizon and more stability for planning.
- **Attractive for Rural Investing**: Rural OZs now receive better benefits, including a 30% basis step-up and more lenient property improvement requirements.

### Cons:

- **Limited Eligibility**: Only capital gains can be invested—not regular income or IRA funds. Critically, you must invest through a QOF to receive any benefit.
- **Tight Geography Rules**: The 2025 law narrowed eligible zones significantly, limiting some previously popular areas like urban tracts in Denver or Boulder. Zones are now re-designated on a rolling 10-year basis.
- **Long-Term Illiquidity**: Funds require a 10+ year commitment to fully realize tax benefits, and many projects are not easily sold early.

- **Complex Compliance**: Strict IRS rules for qualifying investments, reporting, and fund structure must be followed—or the tax benefits are lost.
- **Lack of Diversification**: Many OZ funds are concentrated in a single project, sponsor, and region—this may not suit all investor risk profiles.

## Diversification Approach

We explored the Four Pillars of Passive Investing in Chapter 4. Here's how OZ implements diversification.

- **Geography**: Most OZs just focus on one project in one geography. With the new rules, there is a strong rural focus.
- **Asset Class:** Usually focused on one asset class.
- **Strategy**: Usually focused on one strategy.
- **Sponsor:** Usually one sponsor.

If you have a diverse portfolio of real estate investments, you might not need additional diversification in your next investment. If so, the focused approach of a typical OZ could be a great fit for you. If you have a limited number of real estate investments, this degree of concentration might not be in your best interest.

## Common Pitfalls and Mistakes

- **Missing the 180-Day Window:** You must contribute capital gains within 180 days of realization. Missing the deadline disqualifies the investment from all OZ tax benefits.

- **Investing Ordinary Income:** Only capital gains are eligible for OZ benefits. Contributing ordinary income—even accidentally—voids the tax advantages.
- **Assuming All OZs Are High-Risk Neighborhoods:** While some OZs are in challenged areas, others (like Englewood, Colorado, under the old rules) are quite attractive. However, new rules now prioritize rural and lower-income zones. Always research the local fundamentals, not just the tax incentives.
- **Choosing the Wrong Sponsor or Fund:** Many OZ funds are single-asset and single-sponsor. If the sponsor underperforms, your entire investment is at risk. Additionally, OZs offer no benefit unless held for 10+ years, making fund selection critical.
- **Underestimating IRS Compliance Burden:** OZ funds now have extensive annual reporting obligations, including tract-level job creation data. Failure to comply can trigger up to $50,000 in penalties—so pick sponsors with strong legal and tax teams.
- **Not Doing Detailed Due Diligence:** See Chapter 11 for ideas on this.

## QOZB Rules: Common Deal-Killers

For real estate investors, the Qualified Opportunity Zone Business (QOZB) requirements create the most frequent compliance issues.

### Original Use or Substantial Improvement Test

Property must be either:

- (a) originally placed in service in the OZ by the QOF/QOZB, **OR**

- (b) substantially improved (QOF must invest additional capital equal to or exceeding the building's initial cost basis within 30 months)

**Example:** You buy a building for $1 million ($300K land, $700K building). To qualify, you must invest at least $700K in improvements to the building within 30 months (doubling the building basis). Land basis doesn't count, though land improvements do.

### Triple Net (NNN) Lease Limitations

- A QOZB cannot simply lease property on an NNN basis where the tenant handles all operating expenses.
- The QOZB must conduct active business operations, not passive real estate holding (though a leasing business with some NNN space can still qualify).

### Working Capital Safe Harbor

- Allows QOZBs to hold working capital for up to 31 months (extendable for federally declared disasters).
- Requires written plan and schedule for deployment.
- Funds must be used consistently with that written plan.
- **Document everything**: The written plan is your audit defense.

### 70% Tangible Property Test

- At least 70% of QOZB assets must be tangible property used in the OZ business.
- This limits financial service businesses or businesses with primarily intangible assets.

### Sin Business Prohibition

- Country clubs, racetracks, gambling facilities, liquor stores, and other "sin businesses" under IRC §144(c)(6)(B) are disqualified.

**Key Insight**: 1031 exchanges defer all gain if rules are met and allow indefinite deferral through successive exchanges. OZ defers only the original rolled gain until 12/31/2026 but offers potential permanent exclusion on the QOF investment's appreciation after 10 years. They serve different strategic purposes.

## State Tax Complications

Federal OZ benefits are powerful but remember state tax treatment varies. Some states fully conform to federal OZ provisions, some partially conform, and others don't recognize OZ benefits at all. California (does not conform), New York (decoupled from certain key provisions like deferral/step-ups), and other high-tax states each have their own rules.

Before investing, verify your state's specific treatment. This can significantly affect your after-tax returns, especially if you're a resident of a high-tax state. Consult with a tax advisor familiar with both federal and state OZ rules.

## Closing Thoughts

The updated OZ program is now permanent, more flexible, and driven by data. Its best tax advantages come from staying invested 10 to 30 years, with rural funds offering extra perks. If you have capital gains to invest, this structure provides powerful tax-deferral tools—but it demands careful planning, fund choice, and compliance.

# Chapter 8: Financial Analysis of Your Options

We have often asked ourselves: "Are you running on a treadmill—moving fast but staying in the SAME place?" That is what happens when real estate investors complete one Section 1031 exchange after another. You sell a property, buy another that looks similar, and repeat the cycle. Over time, this routine can feel like it's more about delaying taxes than truly building wealth.

In this chapter, we will explore how this "treadmill" affects your money, your time, and your freedom. We will look at how it works, where it may hold you back, and when it still makes sense. For some investors, staying on this treadmill is the right move. For others, choosing to pay some—or all—of the capital-gains taxes, and investing differently, may open better opportunities. We will compare strategies using actual numbers and real examples.

Here is the good news: sometimes the treadmill is exactly where you want to be—building wealth through tax-deferred compounding. At other times, stepping off the treadmill intentionally can help you accelerate your wealth faster. The key is knowing which situation you are in.

## What You'll Find in This Chapter

### 1. Math of Serial 1031 Exchanges

Learn how repeated exchanges compound benefits over time—and how keeping the same depreciation schedule can eventually reduce your cash flow. While repeating exchanges keeps the IRS at bay, that benefit comes with trade-offs. By not resetting your depreciation schedule, you may risk reducing your cash flow so much that taking the tax hit might be the mathematically smart play.

2. **Depreciation Reset & Cost Segregation**

   When you buy a new property outside a 1031 exchange, you can start a fresh depreciation schedule and use cost segregation to accelerate tax deductions. This reset can boost early cash flow and reduce tax bills. We'll explain both the basics of IRS rules and practical examples. When you sell and pay taxes rather than exchanging, your new property gets a completely fresh depreciation schedule. Every dollar of purchase price becomes depreciable basis (minus land value, of course). This opens the door to aggressive tax strategies. We'll cover the rules and give practical examples.

3. **July 2025 Tax Law Update**

   The July 2025 tax laws might have an impact on your strategy. Understanding the nuances can give you an investing edge. This is also explored in more depth in Appendix 3.

4. **Distribution Comparisons**

   We'll compare numbers:

   - A passive DST (Delaware Statutory Trust) might offer 5-7% annual cash distributions, plus some appreciation (often 2-3% annually), for total annual returns in the 7-10% range.
   - In contrast, some private real estate funds target 12–17% IRRs, often with greater use of depreciation.

5. **10-Year Example Financial Analysis**

   We'll put real numbers to paper:

   - Scenario 1: Do nothing, keep the active rental.
   - Scenario 2: Sell, pay tax, invest in stocks/bonds.

- Scenario 3: Sell, pay tax, invest in Medium-Term Income fund.
- Scenario 4: Sell, 1031 exchange to a DST.
- Scenario 5: Sell, 1031 exchange to a new active investment property.
- Scenario 6: Sell, defer tax with depreciation with new July 2025 tax law, and invest in National Diversified Fund.
- You'll see side-by-side comparisons of returns, cash flow, and flexibility.

6. **Common Pitfalls and Mistakes**

   What can go wrong—missed deadlines, illiquid markets, limited depreciation, advisor biases, estate challenges. You'll learn what to watch out for.

## Guiding Principal

Very high appreciation properties (80-100%) would lean toward 1031 exchange because the tax bill is so heavy that the benefits of alternative investment strategies have a very high hill to climb. Low appreciation properties are ripe for more strategic exits as this chapter outlines. The properties in between require a solid financial analysis and assessment of your needs for liquidity (and/or difficulty finding adequate replacement assets that can qualify for 1031).

## Why This Chapter Matters

A 1031 exchange can be a powerful way to build long-term wealth—if it's part of a thoughtful plan. By the end of this chapter, you'll better understand:

- How staying in the 1031 cycle affects your cash flow, taxes, and freedom.

- When it makes sense to stay on the treadmill—especially for those who value active real estate or have long-term strategies based on continued active management.
- When stepping off—paying taxes, resetting depreciation, and investing passively—might give your portfolio a new boost.

## 1. The Compounding Math of Serial 1031 Exchanges

When you do a 1031 exchange, you move your capital gains tax from one property to the next. That part is clear—you pay the tax later. Perhaps never! But something hidden happens over time. One 1031 exchange after another can slow down how much profit you harvest each year.

Here's why: After a 1031 exchange, the depreciation schedule stays the same—it carries over from the old property. That means you miss out on getting a fresh start with bigger tax deductions. Over several years, that adds up.

Imagine you keep swapping every few years. Each new property only gives a few years of depreciation left. That leads to smaller tax breaks each year. Even though you avoid paying tax right away, your cash flow grows more slowly.

Let's see this with real numbers. Say you bought a $500,000 property ten years ago. You've taken $145,000 in depreciation, leaving 17.5 years on the schedule. If you exchange into a $800,000 property today:

- Your original $355,000 basis ($500,000 - $145,000) continues depreciating over just 17.5 years = $20,286 annual depreciation.
- Only the $300,000 "excess basis" gets a fresh 27.5-year schedule = $10,909 annual depreciation.

- Total annual depreciation: $31,195.

Compare that to buying fresh:

- Full $800,000 basis over 27.5 years = $29,091 annual depreciation.
- BUT with cost segregation, you could accelerate 30% immediately = $240,000 first-year deduction.

That's a $209,000 difference in year-one deductions alone. At a 37% tax rate, you're giving up $77,000 in immediate tax savings to stay in the exchange. Sometimes that makes perfect sense—if you're deferring $200,000+ in gains. But it's worth understanding the trade-off.

## 2. Depreciation Reset & Cost Segregation Benefits

A real perk of a taxable exit (instead of another 1031 exchange) is that you can start over with a fresh depreciation schedule. The IRS usually sets 27.5 years for residential or 39 years for commercial property depreciation. But with cost segregation, you can speed up that schedule.

Cost segregation breaks down building costs into parts like flooring or fixtures and depreciates them faster over 5, 7, or 15 years. Many studies find 20–40% of a property can be depreciated over a shorter period. This front-loads your tax deductions and boosts cash flow in early years.

Even though bonus depreciation rates were phasing out—from 60% in 2025 to 40% in 2026—cost segregation remains valuable for speeding up deductions. Fortunately, the new July 2025 tax law changed this in a positive way (as discussed below).

This "reset" of depreciation means more tax savings earlier, and better returns on your money.

# 3. July 2025 Tax Law Update

## What Just Changed

On July 4, 2025, President Trump signed into law a wide-ranging tax bill often called the "One Big Beautiful Bill". Among its many provisions, one key change affects depreciation rules for real estate investors. (Please also see Appendix 3.)

## Bonus Depreciation Is Fully Restored

Under the new law, the 100% bonus depreciation rule—originally introduced by the 2017 Tax Cuts and Jobs Act—is now fully restored and made permanent. This is a big shift. Before this update, bonus depreciation slowly phased out: from 80% in 2024, to 60% in 2025, and down to zero by 2027.

With bonus depreciation back, property owners can immediately deduct the full cost of eligible assets placed in service starting January 20, 2025.

## Why It Matters for Cost Segregation

This change makes cost segregation studies even more valuable. Cost segregation breaks a property into parts—like flooring, lighting, and landscaping—some of which can be depreciated over 5, 7, or 15 years. With full bonus depreciation, those short-life components can be deducted all at once, bringing large tax savings in the first year.

## New Opportunities for Investors

What does this mean for you:

- A fresh property purchase often includes many assets eligible for 5–15-year schedules.
- With bonus depreciation, you can deduct the full cost up front, boosting early-year cash flow.
- This new schedule reset offers a stronger tax advantage than repeating a 1031 exchange where you inherit the old property's depreciation.

**Bottom Line for Your Analysis**

This tax update strengthens the case for a "taxable exit" strategy. If you sell and pay capital gains—instead of continuing the 1031 exchange path—you can now reset your depreciation, use cost segregation, and take larger deductions early. It gives you more immediate tax relief and better early cash flow.

# 4. Distribution Comparisons

Let's compare how the six main passive real estate strategies differ in returns, tax treatment, and flexibility. Each structure has a different risk/return profile and cash flow strategy (Figure 8-1).

| Return Attribute | DST | TIC | REIT | Passive LLC / Syndication | Opportunity Zone (OZ) | Private Placement / Fund of Funds (FOF) |
|---|---|---|---|---|---|---|
| Cash-on-Cash Return | 4–6% | 4–6% | 3–6% | 0-6%, depends on strategy | 0–5% early; more later | 0-6%, depends on strategy |
| Appreciation | Modest (2–3% annual) | Similar to DST | Embedded into stock price | Often higher, via renovations | Potentially strong over 10+ yrs | Depends on asset mix |
| IRR (Total Return) | 7–10% | 7–10% | Varies widely (5–12%) | 12–18%+ | 10–15% potential (tax-free gain) | 12–16%+ |
| Depreciation Benefits | Yes, limited | Yes, proportional | No (generally) | Yes, often accelerated | Yes (but delayed benefit) | Yes, often accelerated |

**Figure 8-1: Comparison of Passive Strategies**

Some investors will have a strong preference for immediate, predictable cash flow. DST and REIT broadly offer this as a feature, at the tradeoff of (usually) less long-term appreciation.

Some—certainly not all—Syndications, OZ, Private Placements and FOF will offer immediate and predictable cash flow. If so, the Sponsor will certainly highlight that in the offering documents. Most, however, are not focused on a Buy and Hold strategy that lends itself to immediate cash flow. Rather, many rely on Value Add and Development strategies. These investments will optimize long-term growth but usually not offer much (if any) near-term cash flow. Make sure you ask the Sponsor about this to make sure the investment aligns to your needs.

## 5. 10-Year Example Financial Analysis

Many investors initially hesitate to sell when capital gains taxes are involved. To show how the numbers really play out, we'll walk through a ten-year sample analysis using actual figures from an investor we recently helped.

This investor purchased rental property for $187,000 five years ago and did a $9,300 renovation. It has since increased in value to $315,000. Here's how it performed with her last renter:

(Note: Net operating income = NOI.) If you have paid off your mortgage, that is the cashflow from the investment. In her case, she still had a small mortgage at a great interest rate, so the monthly cashflow was $704, or $8448/year.

| | |
|---|---|
| Monthly Rent | $2,045 |
| Vacancy Loss | $102 |
| Opex + MTC | $614 |
| NOI | $1,329 |
| Loan | $625 |
| Monthly Cash | $704 |
| Annual CF | $8,448 |

That last renter didn't leave the property in good condition, so she's deciding between another renovation or just selling it. Let's analyze it, step by step. First, she has about $184,000 in equity.

She thinks she'll have about 2.5% annual appreciation in the future (similar to what we assume for DST). Appreciation in most markets has been a lot higher than that over the past decade. We expect a "reversion to the mean", where we have several years of lower appreciation. We know her annual cashflow is $8,448 after the mortgage payment.

| | |
|---|---|
| Value of Unit | $315,000 |
| Debt | $131,000 |
| Equity | $184,000 |

| Equity | Appreciation | Cash Flow | Total Return | Total Return % |
|---|---|---|---|---|
| **184,000** | **$7,875** | **$8,448** | **$16,321** | **8.9%** |
| | 2.5% | 4.6% | | |

The likely appreciation is the value of the property, $315,000, multiplied by the expected 2.5% annual rate of appreciation, or $7,875. Her total return is appreciation plus the cashflow, or $16,321 per year. Since she has $184,000 in equity, that's an 8.9% annual return on the equity in the rental.

This simple calculation doesn't consider the small amount of principal being paid off on the loan each month, or the tax value of the depreciation write off. That makes the math much easier to follow, and for most investors, it doesn't change the answer.

## DO NOTHING

What will happen if she does nothing?

Her equity of $184,000 will not have any transaction costs (since she is not selling), and there is no capital gain tax bill. The entire amount grows by 8.9% per year. That's a $16,321 increase in year one, as we showed above. In the second year, it had a bigger gain of $17,769. This is compounding interest. You earn 8.9% return on the original equity AND the interest that is re-invested.

| | Do Nothing |
|---|---|
| Equity from Old Rentals | $184,000 |
| Transaction Costs | |
| Capital Gains Tax | - |
| Amount to Invest | $184,000 |
| Annual Return | 8.9% |
| Start Balance | $184,000 |
| Gain Year 1 | $16,321 |
| Balance End Year 1 | $200,321 |
| Gain Year 2 | $17,769 |
| Balance End Year 2 | $218,090 |
| Balance End Year 3 | $237,435 |
| Balance End Year 4 | $258,495 |
| **Balance End Year 5** | **$281,424** |
| | |
| Gain Year 6 | $24,963 |
| Balance End Year 6 | $306,387 |
| Balance End Year 7 | $333,564 |
| Balance End Year 8 | $363,151 |
| Balance End Year 9 | $395,363 |
| **Balance End Year 10** | **$430,433** |

As Einstein reportedly said, compounding interest is the eighth wonder of the world. Stay the course, and the $184,000 of equity today grows to $430,000 in ten years. This is why real estate investment has created so many millionaires.

What if she is tired of being an active investor? She could sell it now that her tenant had moved out. Multiplying the value of the unit, $315,000, by 6% for sales costs, gives an estimated $18,900 of fees. That would include real estate commissions, title fees, and local transaction fees. You'd need to adjust that for your market.

| | |
|---|---|
| Value of Unit | $315,000 |
| Debt | $131,000 |
| Equity | $184,000 |

| | | |
|---|---|---|
| Equity in Current Rentals Before Sales Costs | | $184,000 |
| Sales Costs (Commission, Title, Inspection) | 6% | $18,900 |
| Equity Net of Sales Costs | | $165,100 |

That would consume $18,900 of equity, leaving $165,000 to invest.

We won't bother you with the math here, but she might have capital gains and depreciation recapture tax of $29,700 to pay. Her CPA, of course, would be the final authority on that.

**STOCK MARKET**

Let's imagine she wants to be done with this problem property and invest the proceeds, after paying the tax, in a balanced fund of stocks and bonds. Historically, that has returned around 8.1%.

| | Stock Market |
|---|---|
| Equity from Old Rentals | $184,000 |
| Transaction Costs | ($18,900) |
| Capital Gains Tax | ($29,736) |
| Amount to Invest | $135,364 |
| Annual Return | 8.10% |
| Start Balance | $135,364 |
| Gain Year 1 | $10,964 |
| Balance End Year 1 | $146,328 |
| Gain Year 2 | $11,853 |
| Balance End Year 2 | $158,181 |
| Balance End Year 3 | $170,993 |
| Balance End Year 4 | $184,844 |
| **Balance End Year 5** | **$199,816** |
| | |
| Gain Year 6 | $16,185 |
| Balance End Year 6 | $216,001 |
| Balance End Year 7 | $233,497 |
| Balance End Year 8 | $252,411 |
| Balance End Year 9 | $272,856 |
| **Balance End Year 10** | **$294,957** |

Her $184,000 in equity today would be $135,000 after the tax payment and the sales costs. That $135,000 grows to $295,000 over a decade. She'd make more keeping the property and dealing with the headaches. But the stocks and bonds are effortless to manage, and very liquid—she can access the funds any time she wants. That's not true with real estate, which usually is not liquid.

Which option is better? It depends on her personal situation. For example, if her overall net worth is not high enough to meet her overall financial goals, bearing down and doing the active management work might be the simplest path to achieving her financial goals. On the other hand, if she already has enough money to meet her needs, more time and less stress from passive investing is likely the better choice.

## MEDIUM TERM INCOME

Another option is to sell and invest in our Medium-Term Income fund (MTI), which pays about 12%. (The actual range is 11-13%, and it depends on how much the investor has placed with Ironton).

You can see that after paying the taxes and transaction costs, the nest egg grows to $420,00 over a decade. This is just $10,000 short of the wealth creation if she kept the investment. This is passive and generates a reliable quarterly cash stream she can use for living expenses.

| | MTI Fund |
|---|---|
| Equity from Old Rentals | $184,000 |
| Transaction Costs | ($18,900) |
| Capital Gains Tax | ($29,736) |
| Amount to Invest | $135,364 |
| Annual Return | 12% |
| Start Balance | $135,364 |
| Gain Year 1 | $16,244 |
| Balance End Year 1 | $151,607 |
| Gain Year 2 | $18,193 |
| Balance End Year 2 | $169,800 |
| Balance End Year 3 | $190,176 |
| Balance End Year 4 | $212,997 |
| **Balance End Year 5** | **$238,557** |
| | |
| Gain Year 6 | $28,627 |
| Balance End Year 6 | $267,184 |
| Balance End Year 7 | $299,246 |
| Balance End Year 8 | $335,156 |
| Balance End Year 9 | $375,374 |
| **Balance End Year 10** | **$420,419** |

## DST

The DST is a frequently chosen option. It usually enables total tax deferral, similar to a 1031 exchange to another actively managed property. However, DST is fully passive to the LP (limited partner). This takes the stress off the investors from management. The catch is the returns are lower, and the fees are often higher than other options. We explored this in depth in Chapter 5. For now, let's see how this investment choice compares to the alternatives.

| | DST |
|---|---|
| Equity from old rentals | 184,000 |
| transaction costs | - |
| Cap gains tax | - |
| Amount to invest | 184,000 |
| Annual return | 10.00% |
| Start balance | 184,000 |
| Gain year 1 | 18,400 |
| Balance end year 1 | 202,400 |
| Gain year 2 | 20,240 |
| Balance end year 2 | 222,640 |
| Gain year 3 | 22,264 |
| Balance end year 3 | 244,904 |
| Gain year 4 | 24,490 |
| Balance end year 4 | 269,394 |
| Gain year 5 | 26,939 |
| **Balance end year 5** | **296,334** |
| | |
| Gain year 6 | 29,633 |
| Balance end year 6 | 325,967 |
| Gain year 7 | 32,597 |
| Balance end year 7 | 358,564 |
| Gain year 8 | 35,856 |
| Balance end year 8 | 394,420 |
| Gain year 9 | 39,442 |
| Balance end year 9 | 433,862 |
| Gain year 10 | 43,386 |
| **Balance end year 10** | **477,249** |

The overall wealth generation is attractive—nearly $480,000. In this example, it's a superior choice than to keep a problematic rental.

## OPPORTUNITY ZONE

An Opportunity Zone (OZ) investment will likely look much like a DST. You likely won't be able to refinance mid-project, so your equity will probably be locked up for the duration of the project. You will need to stay in the investment for ten years to get the optimal tax treatment. The long horizon results in a lower ROI (return on investment) for most investors. The tradeoff is that your after-tax returns will probably be better than the DST.

Since every investor's tax situation is so unique, we didn't try to model this. Consult with your CPA.

## 1031 EXCHANGE

Another choice is to sell this rental with problems and low returns. Find another rental to replace it and use a 1031 exchange to link the sales of the properties to defer the gains.

For this example, we assumed the new rental generated a total return of 15.5% a year (appreciation and cash flow after mortgage). The return of the replacement asset(s) you consider could be higher or lower, depending on your market, the asset class(es) you evaluate, their condition, and host of other factors. Your real estate broker will likely be able to give you some guidance on reasonable expectations for your situation.

| | 1031 Exchg |
|---|---|
| Equity from old rentals | 184,000 |
| transaction costs | - |
| Cap gains tax | - |
| Amount to invest | 184,000 |
| Annual return | 15.50% |
| Start balance | 184,000 |
| Gain year 1 | 28,520 |
| Balance end year 1 | 212,520 |
| Gain year 2 | 32,941 |
| Balance end year 2 | 245,461 |
| Gain year 3 | 38,046 |
| Balance end year 3 | 283,507 |
| Gain year 4 | 43,944 |
| Balance end year 4 | 327,451 |
| Gain year 5 | 50,755 |
| **Balance end year 5** | **378,205** |
| | |
| Gain year 6 | 58,622 |
| Balance end year 6 | 436,827 |
| Gain year 7 | 67,708 |
| Balance end year 7 | 504,535 |
| Gain year 8 | 78,203 |
| Balance end year 8 | 582,738 |
| Gain year 9 | 90,324 |
| Balance end year 9 | 673,063 |
| Gain year 10 | 104,325 |
| **Balance end year 10** | **777,388** |

**LONG TERM FUND**

The final option is to sell and invest for the long term in the National Diversified Fund (NDF) offered by Ironton Capital, which targets 17-20% annualized returns after expenses. Bear in mind this isn't an offer to invest, and these are estimated returns. You'd want to consult your investment team to evaluate any investment decision.

A nice feature is that we have two share classes for NDF.

- One share class has a slightly higher preferred return but does not give any depreciation. This tends to be a great choice if you are investing in your IRA or are investing in cash, and you don't need passive losses (check with your CPA to see what's best for your situation).
- The other share class has a slightly lower preferred return and gets all the depreciation.

If you get the depreciation shares, it can usually be used (check with your CPA) to offset some or all your capital gains from the sale of your investment property. In this example, it cut the current tax liability from $29,700 to $20,400. The remaining equity grows over the next decade to an estimated $695,000.

This example assumes the worst-case scenario, that for some reason you cannot take advantage of the July 2025 tax laws.

| | NDF8 | Do nothing |
|---|---|---|
| Equity from old rentals | 184,000 | 184,000 |
| transaction costs | (18,900) | |
| Cap gains tax | (20,370) | - |
| Amount to invest | 144,730 | 184,000 |
| Annual return | 17.00% | 8.9% |
| Start balance | 144,730 | 184,000 |
| Gain year 1 | 24,604 | 16,321 |
| Balance end year 1 | 169,334 | 200,321 |
| Gain year 2 | 28,787 | 17,769 |
| Balance end year 2 | 198,120 | 218,090 |
| Gain year 3 | 33,680 | 19,345 |
| Balance end year 3 | 231,801 | 237,435 |
| Gain year 4 | 39,406 | 21,061 |
| Balance end year 4 | 271,207 | 258,495 |
| Gain year 5 | 46,105 | 22,929 |
| **Balance end year 5** | **317,312** | **281,424** |
| | | |
| Gain year 6 | 53,943 | 24,963 |
| Balance end year 6 | 371,255 | 306,387 |
| Gain year 7 | 63,113 | 27,177 |
| Balance end year 7 | 434,369 | 333,564 |
| Gain year 8 | 73,843 | 29,588 |
| Balance end year 8 | 508,212 | 363,151 |
| Gain year 9 | 86,396 | 32,212 |
| Balance end year 9 | 594,608 | 395,363 |
| Gain year 10 | 101,083 | 35,069 |
| **Balance end year 10** | **695,691** | **430,433** |

The more likely scenario as we write this in November 2025 is that the accelerated depreciation in the July 2025 tax law will enable you to postpone almost all your capital gains and depreciation recapture (check with your CPA!). How does that change the results?

You wind up with about $90,000 in extra return. While the fund returns are the same (estimated here at 17% per year), you have a larger initial balance (since you can defer the tax). This leads to a better ending outcome.

| | NDF8 | Do nothing |
|---|---|---|
| Equity from old rentals | 184,000 | 184,000 |
| transaction costs | (18,900) | |
| Cap gains tax | (1,846) | - |
| Amount to invest | 163,254 | 184,000 |
| Annual return | 17.00% | 8.9% |
| Start balance | 163,254 | 184,000 |
| Gain year 1 | 27,753 | 16,321 |
| Balance end year 1 | 191,007 | 200,321 |
| Gain year 2 | 32,471 | 17,769 |
| Balance end year 2 | 223,478 | 218,090 |
| Gain year 3 | 37,991 | 19,345 |
| Balance end year 3 | 261,470 | 237,435 |
| Gain year 4 | 44,450 | 21,061 |
| Balance end year 4 | 305,919 | 258,495 |
| Gain year 5 | 52,006 | 22,929 |
| **Balance end year 5** | **357,926** | **281,424** |
| | | |
| Gain year 6 | 60,847 | 24,963 |
| Balance end year 6 | 418,773 | 306,387 |
| Gain year 7 | 71,191 | 27,177 |
| Balance end year 7 | 489,965 | 333,564 |
| Gain year 8 | 83,294 | 29,588 |
| Balance end year 8 | 573,259 | 363,151 |
| Gain year 9 | 97,454 | 32,212 |
| Balance end year 9 | 670,712 | 395,363 |
| Gain year 10 | 114,021 | 35,069 |
| **Balance end year 10** | **784,734** | **430,433** |

In this situation, our investor can get out of the headaches of active management, manage her tax liability, and enjoy an entire passive investment that generates a much higher return over time.

### What's the bottom line of these scenarios?

| Comparison of alternatives | Est return | vs. do Nothing |
|---|---|---|
| Do nothing | 430,000 | - |
| Sell + stock/bond market | 295,000 | (135,000) |
| Sell + Ironton income fund | 420,000 | (10,000) |
| Sell + invest in DST | 480,000 | 50,000 |
| Sell + 1031 exchange to 15.5% rental | 780,000 | 350,000 |
| Sell + Ironton long term, limited depreciation | 695,000 | 265,000 |
| Sell + Ironton long term, with July '25 tax law changes | 785,000 | 355,000 |

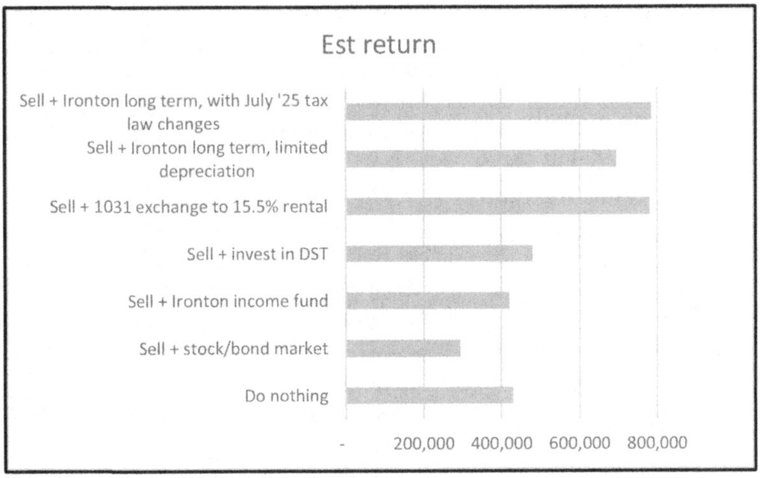


As you can see, a 1031 exchange to another active rental at a 15.5% return achieves about the same wealth generation as the Ironton long-term fund with the July 2025 tax law changes.

- If you can find a replacement property with that return or better, you might be best off to continue the active management path with the 1031 exchange.
- If you are unable to find a replacement with these returns, not only can you make more money with the long-term passive

fund, but you can also free up a lot of your time and reduce stress.

- Alternatively, you might discover that with active management you can generate a higher return. Let's assume over ten years it develops an additional $100,000 of wealth. At that point you and your family can decide if making a little less money is worth trading for potentially less risk (thanks to a diversified portfolio) and less work (since the long-term fund is truly passive). Also, if you, the active manager, become disabled, the management of the property would not become a burden to the other family members.

You and your family now have all the facts needed to make a fully informed business decision.

Would you like to see what these options could look like for your portfolio? Go to http://irontoncapital.com/gopassive to choose the best time for your free portfolio review so you can get all the information to take to your financial advisors. We will re-create this analysis for your unique situation.

# 6. Common Pitfalls and Mistakes

Even well-planned strategies can run into trouble. Here are the most common mistakes investors make—whether they're sticking with 1031 exchanges or considering an exit strategy.

### Missing Critical 1031 Deadlines

As discussed in Chapter 1, the 45-day identification and 180-day closing periods are non-negotiable. Missing these dates means the exchange fails and taxes are due immediately.

## Mishandling Exchange Funds

Also as discussed in Chapter 1, you must use a qualified intermediary (QI) to hold the sale proceeds. If you even temporarily access the funds, your exchange may fail.

## Misreading "Like-Kind" and Boot Rules

Choosing the wrong type of property (e.g., mixing investment with personal property) can invalidate the exchange. Also, forgetting to match or exceed debt on the new property can create "boot"—which triggers immediate tax.

## Rushing Into a DST Without Due Diligence

As we discussed in Chapter 5, DSTs offer simplicity, but not all are the same. Investors sometimes overlook sponsor quality, fee structures, and underlying property risks. A clear review of documents, fees, and sponsor track records can help avoid a bad fit or surprise outcomes.

## Overlooking Cost Segregation Risks

Errors in asset classification or weak documentation can lead to IRS audits. Overly aggressive depreciation in early years may result in recapture later, especially if used in a future 1031 exchange. Failing to hire qualified engineers or maintain records can cancel the benefits of a cost segregation study.

## Skipping Long-Term Planning

A fresh depreciation schedule is great early on but leads to higher future tax recapture unless it matches your long-term goals. That can be fine, but you need an integrated, long-term strategy that takes this into account. A property purchased with cost segregation may need to be held longer to beat depreciation recapture and maximize savings. If you still plan serial exchanges, accelerated depreciation may not match that path.

The recapture of depreciation tax rate depends on what was depreciated—in the case of cost segregation, you are intentionally separating out the personal property, which is taxed up to 37% rather than the real estate recapture at 25%.

**Example**: You do cost segregation on a new $1 million purchase, taking $300,000 in bonus depreciation. If you sell in year 5, you'll recapture that $300,000 at ordinary income rates (up to 37%) rather than the 25% depreciation recapture rate because the $300,000 represents personal property, not real estate as defined by the IRS. But if you hold for 10+ years, the time value of that upfront deduction usually wins. The key is matching your depreciation strategy to your holding timeline.

## Ignoring Liquidity Needs

Serial 1031s tie up capital and limit flexibility. If the market changes fast, you may miss chances or be trapped in unfavorable deals with tight timelines. Exiting with a taxable event, while paying taxes upfront, gives you freedom to act quickly in new opportunities or easier access to cash.

## Underestimating Sponsor and Investment Quality

Whether it's a DST or private fund, sponsor quality and strategy matter. Gimmicky marketing or lack of track record can pose major risks. Annual reviews, operational transparency, and due diligence are key to avoiding low-performing or poorly managed deals.

### How to Avoid These Mistakes

- Use the checklists and reminders in Chapter 1 for deadlines and fund transfers.
- Work with qualified intermediaries, tax professionals, and cost segregation experts.
- Conduct deep due diligence (See Chapter 11) to review sponsor materials, fee schedules, track records, and underlying assets.
- Balance your strategy: Consider timeline flexibility, liquidity needs and estate plans before deciding.

By understanding and avoiding these mistakes, you'll be better equipped to decide whether sticking with a 1031 strategy makes sense for you, or whether an exit and reset approach is the smarter path.

## Closing Thoughts

1. **Don't stay in the treadmill just because it's familiar**—assess whether it still serves your goals.
2. **Understand the real costs**, not just fees, but deadlines, stress, and depreciation limits.
3. **A depreciation reset can boost early income** significantly.
4. **Consider liquidity** as part of your strategy—not every dollar needs to stay in property.
5. **Compare returns clearly**. We looked at multiple scenarios for the choices most investors have.

# Chapter 9: Advanced Strategies

By now, you understand the fundamentals of 1031 exchanges. You know the passive investing alternatives to an exchange. You know the timelines, the like-kind requirements, and how to work with a qualified intermediary. But as you plan your transition from active to passive real estate investment, you'll likely encounter situations that don't fit neatly into the standard exchange model.

- Maybe you need to extract some cash from your properties but still want to defer most of your taxes.
- Perhaps you're thinking about how your real estate fits into your estate plan.
- You might be wrestling with partnership complications that require creative solutions.

This chapter explores these advanced strategies and more—not because they're intellectually interesting (though they can be), but you need to know which tools can make the difference between a good outcome and a great one for your specific situation.

## Partial Exchanges and Strategic Deleveraging

Sometimes a full exchange doesn't align with your goals. You might need cash for another opportunity, want to reduce your debt load, or simply prefer a simpler financial life. A "partial exchange" lets you achieve these objectives while still deferring some or most of your taxes.

## Understanding Boot: The Taxable Portion

In exchange terminology, "boot" is anything you receive that isn't like-kind property. This includes:

- Equity that you don't reinvest
- Debt relief not offset by new debt (or outside cash)
- Non-qualifying assets that you receive in the exchange and that are paid for with your 1031 funds

**Key**: You only pay tax on the boot you receive, not on your entire gain. This creates planning opportunities.

Let's break down how boot is calculated in more detail.

**Cash Boot:** The most straightforward type. If you sell for $1 million and only reinvest $800,000, the difference ($200,000) represents cash boot.

**Mortgage Boot:** More complex. You must replace debt with either new debt or additional cash. If you sell a property with a $600,000 mortgage and buy a replacement with only a $400,000 mortgage, you have $200,000 of mortgage boot unless you invest an additional $200,000 in cash.

**Net Boot Calculation:** The IRS looks at your net position. You can offset mortgage boot with additional cash invested, but you cannot offset cash boot with additional debt assumed.

You don't need to memorize these rules; make sure that you have a general understanding that partial 1031s are possible and offer flexibility. Then work with someone experienced with your specific facts and circumstances.

## Strategic Cash-Out Scenarios

Let's look at several detailed examples of how partial exchanges work in practice.

### Example 1: Planned Partial Cash-Out for Business Investment

Robert owns an apartment building in Phoenix.

- Current value: $3,000,000
- Mortgage balance: $1,000,000
- Original purchase price: $1,400,000
- Improvements over time: $200,000
- Accumulated depreciation: $800,000
- Adjusted basis: $800,000 ($1,600,000 - $800,000)
- Total realized gain if sold: $2,200,000

He wants to transition to passive investing but also needs $500,000 for his daughter's medical practice startup. Here's his detailed strategy:

**The Transaction:**

- Sells for $3,000,000
- Pays off $1,000,000 mortgage
- Closing costs: $180,000
- Net proceeds: $1,820,000
- Reinvests $1,320,000 in a 1031-friendly passive syndication at 50% LTV
- Keeps $500,000 cash

**Tax Calculation:**

- Total realized gain: $2,200,000
- Depreciation recapture (25% rate): $800,000
- Capital gain: $1,400,000
- Boot received: $500,000

Since the boot ($500,000) is less than the total gain ($2,200,000), all boot is taxable:

- First $500,000 is treated as depreciation recapture
- Tax on boot: $500,000 × 25% = $125,000
- Federal tax saved through deferral: approximately $425,000
- Plus state tax savings (varies by state)

## Example 2: Using Passive Losses to Offset Boot

Sandra has been a real estate professional for years and has accumulated $300,000 in suspended passive losses from various properties. She's selling an office building.

- Sale price: $2,500,000
- Mortgage: $1,200,000
- Adjusted basis: $900,000
- Realized gain: $1,600,000

**Her Strategy:**

- Takes $300,000 in cash boot
- Reinvests the remaining proceeds

- Uses suspended passive losses to offset $300,000 gain
- Net tax on boot: $0

This effectively converts tax-deferred passive losses into tax-free cash.

## The Deleveraging Strategy

Many investors approaching retirement want to reduce or eliminate debt. The challenge: paying off debt in an exchange can create taxable boot. Here are several approaches:

### <u>Example 3</u>: Multi-Step Deleveraging Strategy

Susan owns several rental properties.

- Combined value: $4,000,000
- Combined mortgages: $2,400,000 (60% LTV)
- Net equity: $1,600,000
- Combined adjusted basis: $1,500,000
- Total gain if sold: $2,500,000

She wants debt-free passive investments. Here's her sophisticated approach.

**<u>Step 1—Initial Exchange:</u>**

- Sells all properties for $4,000,000
- Identifies DST interests totaling $4,000,000
- Structures with 40% leverage ($1,600,000 debt)
- Invests her $1,600,000 equity plus assumes $1,600,000 of DST debt

- Reduces total debt from $2,400,000 to $1,600,000
- Boot from debt relief: $800,000

**Step 2—Post-Exchange Refinancing (6 months later):**

- DST sponsor offers a refinancing option
- Pays off remaining $1,600,000 debt
- Results in debt-free position
- No tax consequences (loan payoff isn't a taxable event)

**Alternative Approach—Staggered Sales:**

- Year 1: Sells half the portfolio, exchanges into debt-free DSTs
- Year 2: Sells remaining portfolio, exchanges into debt-free DSTs
- Spreads any boot recognition over two tax years
- May benefit from different tax rates or brackets

## When Taking Boot Makes Sense

Sometimes recognizing some gain is the smart move.

### Example 4: State Tax Arbitrage

Michael owns property in California (13.3% top state tax rate) and is moving to Texas (0% state tax).

**California Property**

- Value: $5,000,000
- Basis: $2,000,000
- Gain: $3,000,000

**Option 1—Full exchange while California resident.**

- Defers all federal and California tax
- But California's "clawback" provision means state tax is only deferred, not eliminated

**Option 2—Take $1,000,000 boot after establishing Texas residency.**

- Federal tax on boot (23.8%): $238,000
- California tax: $0 (no longer resident)
- Saves approximately $133,000 in state taxes

## Partial Exchange Planning Checklist

Before executing a partial exchange, work through the following items.

**Financial Analysis:**

- [ ] Calculate total realized gain
- [ ] Determine cash needs
- [ ] Identify suspended passive losses available
- [ ] Project tax on various boot amounts
- [ ] Compare to alternative financing options

**Timing Considerations:**

- [ ] Review current year tax situation
- [ ] Consider next year's projected income
- [ ] Evaluate state residency timeline
- [ ] Plan for estimated tax payments

**Structure Decisions:**

- [ ] Determine optimal boot amount
- [ ] Decide cash vs. debt relief boot
- [ ] Plan replacement property financing
- [ ] Document business purpose for cash

**Professional Coordination:**

- [ ] Review strategy with CPA
- [ ] Confirm QI understands partial exchange
- [ ] Coordinate with estate attorney if applicable
- [ ] Align with financial advisor on cash deployment

# Estate Planning Integration

For many real estate investors, the ultimate tax strategy isn't deferring taxes once—it's eliminating them entirely. The combination of 1031 exchanges and estate planning can help achieve this goal.

**"Step-Up in Basis" (Magic)**

If you hold property until death, your heirs receive a "stepped-up basis" equal to the property's fair market value at the time they inherit the property.

- All your deferred gain disappears.

Let's examine this with a multi-generational case study.

**The Thompson Family Legacy**

- 1975: George Thompson buys farmland for $200,000.
- 1995: Exchanges into apartment building ($2,000,000 value).
- 2010: Exchanges into office complex ($5,000,000 value).
- 2023: Exchanges into diversified, passive portfolio ($12,000,000 value).
- 2024: George passes away.

**Tax consequences:**

- George's total deferred gain: $11,800,000
- Potential tax if sold: ~$3,500,000
- Heirs' stepped-up basis: $12,000,000
- Tax on deferred gain: $0
- Family wealth preserved: $3,500,000

This represents a complete elimination of decades of capital gains tax and depreciation recapture

# Advanced Estate Planning Structures

Beyond simple step-up planning, sophisticated structures can multiply benefits.

### Example 5: The Intentionally Defective Grantor Trust (IDGT) Strategy*

The Williams family has a $10 million real estate portfolio with $7 million in deferred gains.

They want to:

- Continue 1031 exchanges
- Remove assets from taxable estate
- Provide for children and grandchildren

**<u>Their Structure:</u>**

1. Create IDGT with Williams as grantors.
2. Sell properties to IDGT for promissory note.
3. IDGT does 1031 exchange into DSTs (or other eligible assets).
4. Williams pay tax on IDGT income (allowing tax-free growth inside trust).
5. At death, remaining note balance vanishes.

**<u>Results:</u>**

- Assets outside taxable estate
- Continued 1031 deferral
- Tax-free growth for heirs
- Flexibility for future exchanges

**This is an advanced estate-planning strategy that allows an individual (the "grantor") to transfer assets to heirs in a way that significantly reduces estate taxes, while still paying income taxes on the trust's earnings. The trust is intentionally structured to be "defective" for income tax purposes—meaning the grantor pays the income taxes—but effective for estate-tax purposes, excluding those assets from the grantor's taxable estate. You will want to consult with your financial team to see if this applies to your unique situation. Our goal in this book was simply to make you aware of the strategy.*

**Example 6: Charitable Remainder Trust (CRT) with 1031**

Dr. Patel owns medical buildings worth $8 million (basis: $2 million). She wants income for life and a legacy for her medical school.

**Strategy:**

1. Exchanges buildings into passive, 1031-eligible interests
2. After holding period, contributes 1031 assets to CRT
3. CRT sells 1031 interests tax-free
4. Provides 5% annual income for life
5. Remainder to medical school

**Benefits:**

- Immediate charitable deduction: ~$3 million
- Lifetime income: ~$400,000/year
- No capital gains tax
- Estate tax deduction
- Named building at medical school

# Liquidity Strategies During Life

One challenge with the "exchange until death" strategy is accessing cash. (Cash being in higher demand among the living, after all).

Here are some sophisticated approaches.

## Post-Exchange Refinancing

Refinancing the property you want to sell before a 1031 exchange begins is often problematic. This is thankfully less true if you want to refinance the property that you acquire after a 1031 exchange completes.

A refinance doesn't produce taxable income, even after an exchange.

**Example Refinancing Analysis:**

- Property value: $5,000,000
- Conservative LTV: 50%
- Available cash: $2,500,000
- Tax consequence: $0
- Annual debt service (4.5%): $112,500
- Net annual cash flow impact varies by property

## Strategic Installment Sales

Instead of refinancing, consider selling fractional interests:

- Sell 20% interest to children
- Use installment note over 10 years
- Spread tax burden
- Provide retirement income
- Children get appreciation on their portion

# Estate Planning Integration Checklist

**Basic Planning:**

- [] Review current deed/title holding
- [] Confirm compatibility with 1031 rules
- [] Update beneficiary designations
- [] Consider revocable trust for probate avoidance

**Advanced Strategies:**

- [] Evaluate IDGT for estate tax savings
- [] Consider CRT for charitable goals
- [] Review family limited partnership options
- [] Analyze generation-skipping opportunities

**Liquidity Planning:**

- [] Project cash needs over next 10 years
- [] Identify refinancing opportunities
- [] Consider installment sale options
- [] Plan for estate tax payment if applicable

**Professional Coordination:**

- [] Estate attorney drafts documents
- [] CPA models tax implications
- [] Financial advisor integrates with overall plan
- [] QI confirms structure works for exchanges

# Reverse and Improvement Exchanges

Sometimes the standard exchange timeline doesn't work. You might find the perfect replacement property before selling your current one, or you might want to improve a property as part of your exchange. These situations call for more complex structures.

## Reverse Exchanges: Buying Before Selling

In hot markets or with unique opportunities, waiting to sell first can mean missing out. A reverse exchange flips the sequence but requires careful planning and access to additional capital.

Buying before you sell is tricky because the IRS does not allow you to own both the property that you want to sell AND the property that you want to buy at the same time. This makes it difficult to buy first.

To get around this rule, you can have a third party (usually your QI) establish a new LLC called an "Exchange Accommodation Titleholder" to buy the property that you want to buy and hold onto it until your sale takes place. (It is also possible, but less common, to have the Exchange Accommodation Titleholder buy the property that you want to sell instead.)

### <u>Detailed Example</u>: The Mountain View Opportunity

The Johnsons owned a 12-unit building in Denver:

- Current value: $2,400,000
- Mortgage: $1,400,000
- Equity: $1,000,000
- Monthly cash flow: $8,000

A perfect new investment appeared:

- Medical office portfolio
- 7% projected annual return
- $1,000,000 minimum investment
- Closing in 30 days
- Only $3 million remaining availability

Their challenge: Denver winter market meant 3-4 months to sell.

**Reverse Exchange Solution:**

Week 1:

- Engaged Exchange Accommodation Titleholder (EAT)
- EAT formed LLC to acquire Medical portfolio interest
- Secured bridge loan: $1,000,000 at 8% interest (often with a community bank)

Week 4:

- EAT's LLC closed on Medical portfolio investment
- Started receiving monthly Medical portfolio distributions
- Listed Denver property

Month 3:

- Denver property under contract
- Buyer due diligence period

Month 4:

- Closed on Denver property sale

- Paid off bridge loan
- Completed exchange documentation
- EAT transferred Medical portfolio to Johnsons

Total additional costs:

- EAT fee: $8,500
- Bridge loan interest (4 months): $26,667
- Total: $35,167

Worth it? They secured an investment that's now closed to new investors and generating stable passive income.

## Key Reverse Exchange Considerations

### Financing the Purchase

Options when you need capital before selling:

- Outside cash (if you're liquid enough)
- Bridge loans (typically high interest)
- Home equity lines (better rates, personal liability)
- Securities-backed loans (if you have portfolios)
- Partner/private loans (negotiate terms)

## Improvement Exchanges: Building Value

Want to exchange into a property that needs work? An improvement exchange lets construction costs count toward your exchange value—if structured correctly.

The IRS won't let you use your exchange funds to pay directly for improvements or new construction. As they define it, you're not buying real property; rather, you're buying "labor" or "materials", which are not like-kind.

To get around this, we use a similar structure to a reverse 1031 exchange—set up an EAT, let it hold title to the new property, and then wait until the improvements are complete before formally acquiring it through the 1031 exchange.

**Detailed Example: The Warehouse Conversion**

Martinez sold a retail center for $3,000,000 and found a warehouse to convert to creative office space.

- Warehouse purchase price: $2,300,000
- Planned improvements: $700,000
- Total investment: $3,000,000

**The Timeline Reality:**

Days 1-30:

- EAT acquires warehouse
- Finalizes construction contracts
- Permits already in hand (critical!)
- Construction begins

Days 31-90:

- Demolition complete
- Framing and systems underway

- Weekly progress monitoring
- Paying contractors from exchange funds

Days 91-150:

- Substantial completion
- City inspections
- Punch list items
- Racing against deadline

Day 165:

- Construction complete
- Final lien waivers obtained
- Property transfers to Martinez
- Exchange completed successfully

**What Made It Work:**

- Permits secured before starting exchange
- Experienced contractor with bond
- Conservative timeline (planned for 150 days)
- Weekly oversight meetings
- Contingency fund for surprises

## Improvement Exchange Pitfalls and Solutions

**<u>Common Failure Points:</u>**

- Permit Delays
  - <u>Solution</u>: Secure all permits before closing
  - Have backup properties identified
- Contractor Problems
  - <u>Solution</u>: Require performance bonds
  - Have multiple bid alternates ready
- Scope Creep
  - <u>Solution</u>: Detailed plans in identification
  - No changes after day 45
- Weather/Unforeseen Delays
  - <u>Solution</u>: Build 30-day buffer
  - Consider inside work only

## Reverse and Improvement Exchange Checklist

**<u>Reverse Exchange Planning:</u>**

- [ ] Calculate bridge financing needs
- [ ] Secure financing commitments
- [ ] Interview experienced EATs
- [ ] Model carrying costs
- [ ] Prepare old property for quick sale
- [ ] Have backup sale strategies

**Improvement Exchange Planning:**

- [ ] Obtain all permits pre-closing
- [ ] Complete construction drawings
- [ ] Secure contractor bids and bonds
- [ ] Build 30+ day timeline buffer
- [ ] Arrange construction monitoring
- [ ] Prepare detailed identification

**Cost-Benefit Analysis:**

- [ ] Compare to standard exchange options
- [ ] Model additional costs vs. benefits
- [ ] Consider risk factors
- [ ] Evaluate alternative properties
- [ ] Confirm team experience level

## Drop and Swap Strategies

When partners want to go separate ways, the path to individual 1031 exchanges gets complicated. Recall the Same Taxpayer Rule referenced in Chapter 1. It's not possible to have one taxpaying entity start a 1031 exchange and have a separate individual/entity complete the exchange by buying the replacement property.

The "drop and swap" strategy—distributing property from a partnership to partners before an exchange—is a very common way to route around this issue. Unfortunately, it faces significant IRS scrutiny.

## The Partnership Dilemma—Detailed Analysis

Let's examine why this is so challenging through a detailed case study:

### Case Study: The Riverside Partners Dissolution

Riverside LLC owns three apartment complexes:

- Property A: $4 million value (downtown location)
- Property B: $3 million value (suburban)
- Property C: $3 million value (suburban)
- Total value: $10 million
- Total debt: $6 million
- Total equity: $4 million

Three equal partners:

- Adams: Wants to exchange into DSTs (passive)
- Baker: Wants to exchange into active properties
- Carter: Wants to cash out for retirement

**Option 1: Partnership Exchanges (Swap and Drop)**

- Riverside LLC sells all properties.
- Riverside LLC acquires replacement properties.
- Later distributes different assets to partners.
- Problem: Carter has to wait for cash.

**Option 2: Drop and Swap**

- Distribute properties to partners as TIC.
- Each partner sells their interest.
- Each does their own exchange (or not).
- Problem: Potential IRS scrutiny if not executed correctly.

**Option 3: Hybrid Approach**

- Adams and Baker buy out Carter now.
- LLC continues with two partners.
- Later exchange and split.
- Problem: Requires significant capital.

## Strategic Alternatives to Drop and Swap

### 1. Installment Sale to Accommodating Partners

Structure:

- Carter sells partnership interest to Adams and Baker
- Uses installment note over 5+ years
- Adams and Baker then exchange
- Spreads Carter's tax burden

Benefits:

- Clean partnership continuity
- Predictable tax consequences
- Flexibility for all parties

### 2. Special Allocations Strategy

If partnership agreement allows:

- Allocate more cash/boot to exiting partner
- Allocate more property to exchanging partners
- Must have "substantial economic effect"
- Requires careful tax planning

### 3. Delaware Statutory Trust Conversion

<u>Sophisticated Approach:</u>

- Convert partnership to DST before sale.
- DST interests qualify for 1031 treatment.
- Partners can exchange DST interests.
- Avoids drop and swap risks.

## Drop and Swap Risk Assessment Checklist

### Evaluate Your Risk Level

**<u>High Risk Factors (Avoid if multiple are present):</u>**

- [ ] Buyer already identified
- [ ] Sale within 6 months of distribution
- [ ] No business purpose documented
- [ ] Partners not truly independent
- [ ] California property involved
- [ ] Prior IRS audit history

**Risk Mitigation Strategies:**

- [ ] Wait 12+ months after distribution
- [ ] Document business disagreements
- [ ] Partners make independent decisions
- [ ] Separate property management
- [ ] Different insurance policies
- [ ] Independent tax returns filed

**Documentation Requirements:**

- [ ] Partnership resolution for distribution
- [ ] Business purpose memorandum
- [ ] Independent decision records
- [ ] Separate bank accounts
- [ ] Individual property tax bills
- [ ] Arms-length written agreements

**Professional Planning:**

- [ ] Tax opinion letter obtained
- [ ] All partners separately represented
- [ ] Structure reviewed by litigator
- [ ] Insurance advisor consulted
- [ ] Alternative structures modeled

## Closing Thoughts

The path from active to passive real estate investing doesn't have to be straight. These advanced strategies give you the flexibility to address your unique situation while maximizing tax benefits.

Remember:

- Every dollar of tax deferred can be invested for your future.
- Complexity requires competent professional guidance.
- The best strategy aligns with your life goals, not just tax goals.
- Time and planning prevent most problems.

Use these tools wisely, always with professional guidance, and with a clear understanding of both the opportunities and the risks they present.

For 1031 exchange guidance, visit https://1031x.com

In our next chapter, we'll explore how to build and work with the professional team that can help you execute these strategies successfully. The difference between success and failure often comes down to the quality of your advisors and how well you work together.

# Chapter 10: Your Advisory Dream Team

Transitioning from active to passive real estate investing—whether through 1031 exchanges into DSTs, private equity funds, or other passive vehicles—requires more than just good intentions and available capital. You need a carefully assembled team of professionals who:

- Understand the technical requirements
- Can guide you through strategic implications
- Move and communicate responsively (timing matters)

When you were actively managing rental properties, you might have gotten by with a basic CPA who handled your simple Schedule E, a real estate agent who occasionally helped you buy or sell, and perhaps a general practice attorney for the odd contract issue.

That approach won't cut it when you're dealing with more complex issues, more complex properties, and your hands are off the wheel.

This chapter provides a roadmap for assembling and working effectively with five critical advisor types: Qualified Intermediaries, real estate attorneys, CPAs specializing in real estate, experienced brokers, and fund sponsors. Each plays a distinct but interconnected role in your success.

## Qualified Intermediary

### Role and Critical Importance

Your Qualified Intermediary is the linchpin of any 1031 exchange. They're not just holding your money—they're the conductor ensuring every step of your exchange happens in harmony and compliance with IRS requirements.

The QI's fundamental job is preventing you from taking "constructive receipt" of your sale proceeds, which would immediately disqualify your exchange and trigger full tax liability. But experienced QIs do much more.

A good QI will:

- Guide you through IRS timelines
- Coordinate with other parties
- Prepare required documentation
- Often serve as the voice of reason when deal pressure mounts.

Here's what many investors don't realize: **the IRS provides no safety net for QI mistakes**. If your intermediary mishandles funds or fails to follow procedures correctly, you bear the tax consequences.

If you're contemplating a 1031 exchange, QI selection is perhaps your most critical decision in the entire exchange process.

### What to Look for in a QI

- **Deep 1031 Experience**: This should be obvious. The best modern Qualified Intermediaries are comprised of teams of legal, tax, real estate, and investment experts. They've handled 1031s for years, sometimes decades, and should have a track record you can scrutinize.
- **Financial Stability and Security Measures**: You'll be entrusting potentially millions of dollars to this entity. Verify they maintain segregated qualified escrow or trust accounts (your money should never commingle with their operating funds or other clients' money). They should carry substantial fidelity bonds and additional

insurance, and preferably undergo annual audits. In an age of significant wire fraud in the real estate industry, check to make sure they have adequate cybersecurity and wire protocols.

- **Transparent Fee Structure**: Reputable QIs normally charge flat fees for standard exchanges—typically $800-$1,500. Be wary of hidden charges or QIs who won't clearly detail their fee structure upfront. They should earn their fee through successful completion, not by nickel-and-diming you throughout the process.
- **Professional Credentials**: While not required by law, look for QIs with Certified Exchange Specialist (CES®) designations or Federation of Exchange Accommodators (FEA) membership. These indicate commitment to ongoing education and industry best practices.
- **Reviews and Reputation**: Look up the QI's reviews on Google, Facebook, or investor-specific forums like BiggerPockets.

### Smart Questions to Ask Potential QIs

- **"Can you walk me through your fund security measures and provide details about your insurance coverage?"**

  They should readily explain segregated accounts, daily reconciliation procedures, and insurance limits.

- **"What happens if I can't complete my exchange?"**

  A client-focused QI will acknowledge that sometimes paying tax is better than making a bad investment, and they'll explain their procedures for returning unused funds.

- **"Have any of your clients ever failed an IRS or state audit due to an exchange issue?"**

  While audits of 1031s are rare, they do happen. Errors on the part of the 1031 exchange provider are indefensible; errors on the part of their client are sometimes still the fault of poor communication and expectation-setting on behalf of the QI.

### Red Flags to Avoid

- **Commingled Funds**: Any QI that can't clearly explain how your money stays segregated from their operating funds and other clients' money should be immediately disqualified.
- **Unusually Low Fees**: A dramatically cheaper QI might be cutting corners on insurance, security measures, or expertise. This is not the place to bargain hunt.
- **Limited Experience**: If they can't provide specific examples of handling exchanges similar to yours, or if 1031s represent a small part of their business, look elsewhere.
- **Poor Communication**: If they're hard to reach or unclear in explanations during the courtship phase, expect worse during the stress of an actual exchange.

## Real Estate Attorneys

### Do You Need Specialized Legal Counsel?

QIs handle exchange mechanics, but real estate attorneys are sometimes needed to properly structure the underlying transactions. They review and draft contracts, address title issues (depending on the state you're in), handle entity structuring considerations, and serve as your advocate when disputes arise.

This becomes especially critical in complex situations: partnership exchanges, multi-state transactions, or deals involving fund sponsors and private placements. The legal nuances can make or break your exchange, and the IRS **does not permit** your QI to provide legal advice.

### Key Attributes for Real Estate Exchange Attorneys

- **1031 Exchange Expertise**: Your attorney should have direct experience with exchanges, not just general real estate law. They should understand the interplay between exchange requirements and contract terms.
- **Attention to Detail**: Exchange failures can stem from seemingly minor documentation errors. If you have a complicated sale or are working with a large portfolio, a good attorney will double-check the work of the title company, qualified intermediary, etc.
- **Tax Law Understanding**: While they don't need to be tax attorneys, they should understand how exchange mechanics interact with depreciation recapture, basis calculations, and estate planning considerations.

### Critical Questions for Attorney Candidates

- **"How many 1031 exchange transactions have you handled, and can you describe a challenging situation you successfully navigated?"**

  Look for specific examples demonstrating problem-solving skills under exchange constraints.

- **"What activities do you bill for?"**

  Some attorneys bill for reading emails—even emails that you don't send. We've seen attorneys bill 1031 exchange clients because the Exchange Officer at the Qualified Intermediary sent them an email with a simple update. Avoid getting nickel-and-dimed.

- **"How do you coordinate with my other advisors during the exchange process?"**

  The best attorneys actively collaborate with your QI, CPA, and other team members rather than working in isolation. This can be overdone; some attorneys will slow down closing processes unnecessarily due to inexperience, hyper vigilance, or to increase billable work.

### Attorney Red Flags

- **Limited 1031 Knowledge**: If they can't explain basic exchange requirements or seem unfamiliar with IRS deadlines, find someone else. You don't want your lawyer learning 1031s on your transaction.
- **Poor Communication**: If they're slow to respond during the selection process, expect worse when you're racing against exchange deadlines.
- **Overstepping Boundaries**: Be cautious of attorneys who try to provide tax advice beyond their expertise or attempt to act as investment advisors without proper licensing.

## CPAs: Your Tax Strategist

### The CPA's Role in Exchange Success

Most CPAs serve as scorekeepers and paper-filer for standard 1031 exchanges; they want to collect the correct documents at the end, double-check the math, and file your Form 8824 correctly.

Sometimes, however, your CPA is the lynchpin to reinvestment success.

Before you sell, your tax advisor can help determine whether an exchange makes sense in the first place. They can calculate potential tax liability and project long-term implications. During the exchange, they help ensure proper reporting and compliance. After completion, they track your carryover basis and deferred gains for future planning.

In our experience navigating 1031s, good CPAs often know more about the subject property(ies) than the actual owner. Their knowledge helps both the taxpayer and the Qualified Intermediary avoid tripwires that could result in major tax issues.

## What Defines an Exceptional Real Estate CPA

- **Real Estate Specialization**: Tax law is vast and complex. You want a CPA who focuses on real estate investors and understands passive activity loss rules, depreciation methods, Section 1031 nuances, and how these interact with your overall tax situation.
- **1031 Reporting Expertise**: They should be fluent in Form 8824 preparation and understand how to calculate and track carryover basis, deferred gains, and depreciation schedules that span multiple properties over many years.
- **Strategic Tax Planning**: The best CPAs don't just record history—they help you plan ahead. They should model different scenarios (exchange vs. sell and pay tax, DST vs. direct ownership, etc.) and help align tax decisions with your long-term goals.
- **Multi-State Knowledge**: If you invest across state lines, your CPA must understand varying state tax treatments of exchanges. Some states have complex reporting requirements for out-of-state exchange gains. Some states, like Hawai'i, California, and New York are notoriously difficult to work with.

## Essential CPA Interview Questions

- **"How many real estate investors do you work with, and what percentage of your practice focuses on real estate?"**

  You want someone for whom real estate taxation is bread and butter, not an occasional specialty.

- **"Can you explain how you track carryover basis and deferred gains from 1031 exchanges?"**

  They should describe systematic approaches using software or detailed worksheets, not ad-hoc methods.

- **"If I wanted to invest passively in DSTs or private equity funds, how would you handle the tax reporting?"**

  They should understand the structure of different reinvestment options, K-1s, and passive loss implications.

### CPA Warning Signs

- **Limited Real Estate Knowledge**: If they're unfamiliar with basic concepts like passive loss rules or depreciation recapture, they might cost you money through missed opportunities or compliance errors.
- **Poor Record Keeping**: It's impossible to overstate how important this is. If they can't clearly explain how they'll track your exchange basis and deferred gains over time, expect problems down the road.
- **Aggressive or Questionable Advice**: Some professionals don't set and enforce boundaries, either because they're too polite or because they never want to turn away business. Be wary of CPAs pushing dubious strategies or suggesting non-compliance with clear requirements. The risks aren't worth the potential savings.

## Real Estate Brokers

### The Broker's Role in Exchange Transactions

In 1031 exchanges, brokers must work within the compressed timelines and specific requirements that exchanges demand. This means pricing your relinquished property for quick sale while maximizing value, identifying suitable replacement properties before your 45-day deadline, and coordinating with your QI throughout the process.

Very few brokers are 1031 experts. Very few are experts in GP/LP investments, DTSs, or other private equity options. If you are exploring these options and can't find the right broker, you may want to broaden your search to include more financial advisors or RIAs.

### Key Broker Qualifications

- **1031 Exchange Experience is a Bonus**: If your broker understands exchange timelines and requirements, that's a useful bonus. In most 1031 exchange scenarios, however, the broker's main role is to either introduce you to a good Qualified Intermediary and/or to solicit the QI's advice on navigating the 1031 correctly.
- **Market Expertise**: Match your broker's specialization to your needs. Use common sense; if you're selling commercial property, work with commercial specialists.
- **Network and Resources**: Given exchange time constraints, brokers with extensive networks and off-market deal flow provide crucial advantages. For DST brokers, breadth of sponsor relationships means more options for suitable investments.

### Smart Broker Interview Questions

- **"How many 1031 exchanges have you been involved with?"**

  Experience with exchange pressure is, again, helpful but not always necessary.

- **"I'm interested in reinvesting into _____. Do you work in these areas often?"**

  This should be routine territory, not something they need to learn on your transaction.

### Broker Red Flags

- **Limited 1031 Knowledge**: If you're explaining exchange requirements to your broker rather than the reverse, find someone else or instruct them to work very closely with your QI.
- **High-Pressure Tactics**: As always, be wary of brokers pushing specific properties or DSTs without sound reasoning, especially if they seem more interested in their commission than your objectives.
- **Poor Communication**: Time kills deals, especially in exchanges. Slow response times or disorganization during selection indicate bigger problems ahead.

## Fund Sponsors: Investment Partners

### Understanding the Sponsor Relationship

When you exchange into DSTs or invest in private equity real estate funds, you're essentially choosing a sponsor to steward your investment for years. Unlike other advisors who work for you, sponsors are more like business partners—your returns depend on their competence, integrity, and alignment with your interests.

This makes sponsor due diligence critical. Once you invest, you typically have little control, especially in DSTs where investor rights are severely limited by IRS requirements.

### Essential Sponsor Evaluation Criteria

- **Track Record and Performance**: This is paramount. Investigate the sponsor's history with similar investments. How many deals have they completed? What returns did they deliver versus projections? A sponsor consistently meeting or exceeding projections demonstrates conservative underwriting and execution skills.
- **Team Experience and Expertise**: Beyond past performance, consider the team's qualifications. How long have key principals been in real estate? Do they have relevant experience in the asset classes they're offering? Have they successfully navigated different market cycles?
- **Financial Strength**: The sponsor should be well-capitalized with sufficient resources to support investments if needed. Some sponsors co-invest their own funds—an excellent sign of aligned interests.
- **Fee Structure and Alignment**: Evaluate how sponsors earn money and whether their interests align with yours. Reasonable, clearly disclosed fees combined with performance-based components (they do well only if you do well) are positive signs.
- **Transparency and Communication**: Before investing, assess their willingness to answer tough questions and provide detailed information. After investing, good sponsors provide regular updates showing property performance, occupancy, financials, and any issues.

### Critical Sponsor Due Diligence Questions

Note: Take a look at Chapter 11 for more information, as well.

- **"Can you provide details on your track record, specifically prior offerings similar to this one and their outcomes?"**

  Demand hard data, not vague assurances.

- **"What is your skin in the game on this deal? Are you co-investing equity alongside investors?"**

  Sponsor investment aligns interests and provides cushion if things go wrong.

- **"Walk me through all fees and compensation you'll receive and explain how this compares to industry standards."**

  Transparency here is essential.

- **"What are the key risks you see in this investment, and how are you mitigating them?"**

  Trustworthy sponsors readily discuss risks and mitigation strategies.

- **"Does your offering work with 1031 exchanges?"**

  A lot of syndications and PE-sponsored deals are not set up to accept 1031 exchange investor capital. There are real challenges for fund sponsors to navigate in order to be compliant with 1031 rules, and many sponsors elect to forgo the ability to accept 1031 capital.

### Sponsor Red Flags

- **Lack of Track Record or Evasiveness**: If they won't or can't show a performance history, you're betting on unproven management.

- **Overly Optimistic Projections**: Returns significantly above market averages without clear justification often indicate aggressive underwriting designed to sell deals rather than deliver results.
- **High Leverage or Risky Structures**: Excessive debt or complex financing arrangements amplify risks. Be especially wary of floating-rate debt without proper hedging.
- **Conflicts of Interest**: While some conflicts are normal and acceptable if disclosed, be cautious of arrangements where sponsors can profit even if investors lose money.

# Building an Integrated Team

## The Power of Coordination

The most successful 1031 exchanges (and passive investment transitions) happen when multiple advisors work together carefully.

This coordination doesn't happen automatically—it requires advisors who understand their roles and respect others' expertise, plus your active management to ensure everyone stays aligned.

## Managing Your Team Effectively

- **Set Clear Expectations**: At the outset, ensure each advisor understands the overall strategy, timeline, and their specific responsibilities. Provide contact information for all team members and encourage direct communication when appropriate.
- **Facilitate Communication**: Don't make yourself the sole conduit for information. Allow your QI to speak directly with your attorney about contract requirements (although check to make sure about billing first!), or your CPA to discuss tax implications with your broker.

- **Stay Engaged**: While you're building a team to handle complexity, you remain the decision-maker. Stay informed about progress, ask questions when something doesn't make sense, and make decisions promptly when required.
- **Plan for Contingencies**: Discuss backup plans with your team. What if your replacement property falls through on day 40? What if title issues arise? Having contingency plans prevents panic decisions.

### The Investment in Professional Expertise

Quality professional guidance isn't cheap, but it's invariably less expensive than the mistakes that result from inadequate counsel. A skilled QI might charge $1,500 for an exchange that defers $300,000 in taxes. An experienced attorney's $5,000 fee pales in comparison to the cost of a disqualified exchange. A specialized CPA's strategic guidance can save multiples of their annual fees through optimized tax planning.

View these professional fees not as costs but as investments in successful wealth transition. The goal isn't to minimize advisory fees—it's to maximize the value and security of your real estate wealth transformation.

## Closing Thoughts

The transition from active to passive real estate investing represents a fundamental shift in how you build and preserve wealth. It's complex enough that trying to navigate it alone, or with inadequate professional guidance, is both risky and usually counterproductive.

Take time to build this team thoughtfully. Interview multiple candidates for each role. Check references. Ask hard questions. The few extra weeks you spend assembling the right team will pay dividends throughout your wealth-building journey.

**Remember:** In active real estate investing, you could often fix mistakes through better management, additional capital, or time. In passive investing, especially through 1031 exchanges, the stakes are higher and the room for error much smaller. Your advisory team is your insurance policy against costly mistakes and your engine for optimized outcomes.

For 1031 exchange guidance, visit https://1031x.com

# Chapter 11: Due Diligence and Sponsor Evaluation

Now that you know a lot more about 1031 exchanges and the different alternatives, let's review how to get started. Whether you are going to directly invest in a syndication, leverage an Opportunity Zone or Delaware Statutory Trust, or invest in a diversified passive fund, there are common due diligence steps.

## Pre-Planning Activities

It is important to plan before you act.

### Activities Within Your Family.

- Decide if real estate investment is right for your portfolio.
- Decide if you want to invest passively or actively.

See Chapter 8 for a detailed financial analysis comparison of options.

### Activities With Your Advisors.

Talk to your advisory team—most importantly your CPA, but also your attorney and financial advisor if you have them.

#### CPA:

- Tax considerations
- For example, if you have the option to get more passive losses through depreciation, how much would you want?

**<u>CPA or Financial Advisor</u>:**

- For example, which investments should be purchased with cash, versus through your self-directed IRA?
- Does it matter if you personally own the investment, or is there a tax benefit to another method, such as a trust?

**<u>Attorney</u>:**

- How to hold title (for example, in concert with the rest of your estate plan).
- Detailed review of specific fund documents when you are about to invest.

See Chapter 10 for a detailed plan for building your advisor team.

### Activities with Potential Fund General Partners and/or Sponsors

- See how their fund(s) fit your requirements.
- See Chapter 10 for considerations and questions for the GP.

## Due Diligence – Eight Considerations

We recommend reviewing the following eight factors with your financial team when planning your investments.

1. Ask about the **<u>tax</u>** implications of real estate investments, including deductions, depreciation, and potential capital gains taxes.

2. Discuss the investment's **<u>alignment</u>** with your financial goals and risk tolerance.

3. Ask about the **expected returns**, including both income and appreciation potential, as well as any associated fees or expenses.

4. Ask about their **track record** with similar investments.

5. Inquire about the investment's **liquidity** and exit strategies in case you need to sell your stake.

6. Seek clarification on the **due diligence** process, including property evaluations and management procedures, to ensure the investment aligns with your overall financial plan and objectives.

7. Finally, when it is time to make the investment, check with your advisors on how to **hold title**.

8. **Fund** the investment.

Let's spend a moment exploring each facet of the pre-planning and due diligence process.

## 1. Tax Implications

Real estate investments come with various tax implications that can impact your financial outcomes.

- Deductions such as mortgage interest, property taxes, and operating expenses can help reduce taxable income from real estate investments.
- Depreciation allows you to deduct a portion of the property's cost each year to reflect its wear and tear, lowering your taxable income further. This does not apply to REIT (real estate investment trust) but does apply to most other options.
- Additionally, when you sell a property, you may be subject to capital gains taxes on any profits earned.

- However, certain tax strategies, such as 1031 exchanges or investing through tax-advantaged accounts, can help mitigate capital gains taxes.

Understanding these tax implications and seeking guidance from a CPA or financial advisor can optimize your tax efficiency and overall investment returns in real estate.

**Example—Ironton Capital**

- The National Diversified Fund (NDF) will have an option to generate depreciation can be used to offset capital gains and/or passive losses with other investments.
- The Short-Term Income Fund (STI) is taxed as a REIT (Real Estate Investment Trust). For most investors, that is a lower tax bracket than their marginal ordinary income rate.
- Check http://irontoncapital.com/gopassive to learn more about how our funds might help with your situation.

**Example—With 1031 Exchange:**

- Check with your CPA, but you will likely be able to defer your capital gain and depreciation recapture.
- Make sure you understand how your basis will reset, and how that will impact (if at all) future year deductibility of interest.
- If you cannot find an appropriate exchange property in the 45-day identification period, what are your backup plan(s)?

**Example—With DST or OZ:**

- Check with your CPA, but you will likely be able to defer your capital gain and depreciation recapture.

- Make sure you understand how your basis will reset, and how that will impact (if at all) future year deductibility of interest.
- How long will you have to hold the replacement investment to get the most optimal tax handling?

Many financial advisors have deep training and extensive experience with stocks and bonds, but very little exposure to real estate. As a result, they often will be reluctant to offer much advice on real estate as it may be seen as a higher risk to them. Only you can decide, but usually the CPA is the better resource. That leaves this set of activities to be led nearly exclusively by the passive investor.

## 2. Alignment with Goals

When considering an investment's alignment with your financial goals and risk tolerance, it's essential to assess how it fits into your overall financial plan and creating generational wealth.

- Evaluate whether the investment helps you achieve specific objectives, such as building wealth, generating passive income, or diversifying your portfolio.
- Consider your risk tolerance, or how comfortable you are with potential fluctuations in the investment's value.
- Higher-risk investments may offer the potential for greater returns but also come with increased uncertainty and volatility.
- Conversely, lower-risk investments may provide more stability but offer lower potential returns.

**Example—Ironton Capital**

- The National Diversified Fund (NDF) will have dozens of properties in a diverse portfolio. As a result, it'll likely have a lower risk but have less opportunity to achieve above (or below) its 17-20% annual target return. Of course, prior performance is not a predictor of future performance.

- Ironton's income funds like Short Term Income (STI) and Medium-Term Income (MTI) are based on hundreds (or more) of small debt instruments, which really diversifies risk.
- Consult with your financial advisors as you evaluate options from us or other private equity funds.
- Check http://irontoncapital.com/gopassive to learn more about how our funds might help with your situation.

**Example—With 1031 Exchange:**

- Another actively managed property may have one of the best opportunities among the different options for the highest return. It will certainly give you the most control.
- If you enjoy Value-Add or Development, this structure might be optimal.
- The tradeoff is that it's a lot more work for you and might concentrate your risk (lack of diversification).

**Example—With DST or OZ:**

- These options will likely be lower risk and lower return vs. other options.
- If you already have amassed enough wealth to achieve your goals, and capital preservation is now the priority, these could be great ideas.

By aligning the investment with your financial goals and risk tolerance, you can make decisions that suit your individual circumstances and aspirations while balancing potential rewards and risks.

This set of activities is mostly led by the passive investor. The Sponsor or GP (General Partner) will be able to provide some input to you and your advisory team.

## 3. Returns

When inquiring about expected returns for a real estate investment, it's crucial to consider both income and appreciation potential.

- Income refers to the regular cashflow generated from the investment, such as rental payments from tenants.
- Understanding the expected rental income helps assess the investment's ability to generate ongoing returns.
- Appreciation potential refers to the property's expected increase in value over time. This could come from factors like improvements to the property or overall market trends.
- Additionally, you should inquire about any associated fees or expenses, such as property management fees, maintenance costs, or administrative expenses.

Understanding these factors allows you to evaluate the investment's overall profitability and ensure it aligns with your financial goals.

**Example—Ironton Capital**

- NDF is designed to have minimal income and have most of the returns characterized as long-term capital gains. NDF is not liquid and requires a 4–6-year commitment.
- STI is designed to have maximum liquidity and has tax-preferred treatment as a REIT. Principal preservation is a high priority. As a result, it has lower returns in the 8-9% range with predictable quarterly dividends.

- MTI has an intermediate level of liquidity, and accordingly, an intermediate level of returns. The target is 11-13% annually, paid in equal quarterly installments.
- All these return projections are net of all fees.

**Example—With 1031 Exchange:**

- Your returns will vary depending on the choice of your next project. You can pick low risk, low involvement, low return all the way to high risk, high effort and (hopefully) high returns. You are in control.

**Example—With DST or OZ:**

- Usually, lower risk and lower returns than other options.
- Set-up fees may be higher than some other options.
- Be sure to understand if placement commissions are due.

This set of activities is initiated by the Sponsor or the GP. They should have a very detailed business case, examining several economic scenarios. If not, that is a red flag. If you have the business skills, time, and interest, ask for a copy of the XLS (Microsoft Excel) model. If you lack the skills and have a family member or business associate you trust who loves Excel, consider enlisting such help.

Ask the Sponsor to show you the high points of the model and how it works. Find out which variables have the most impact on the profit. For developing a new apartment complex, you might find these variables are most impactful:

- Rents and occupancy rates upon completion
- Finishing on time and on budget
- Assumptions for the sales price when complete and stabilized

Ask the Sponsor to share the research they used to guide the assumptions in the model.

For example:

- What rents are comparable existing apartment complexes near the new project getting? How do the amenities and features of this project compare? Since yours will be new and shiny, your project will usually outperform similar but dated properties nearby.
- What is the Sponsor's track record for construction management on prior projects with a similar scope? Is there a fixed cost bid for the construction? Does this local government have a good reputation for being business friendly and expediting the permitting and construction approval process?
- What prices have recent sales of similar projects sold for in the current market? Are the assumptions of the sale reasonable in comparison?

Ask how the Sponsor/GP has managed these key variables in the past. This isn't nosy or "bad behavior" on your part. A good Sponsor will welcome these questions from a passive investor. If you are curious and have a passion for this, explore this in depth; it will be the most time-consuming element for you. If you are not that curious, it's ok to review this at a high level if you otherwise feel comfortable with the Sponsor.

## 4. Track Record

Be sure to ask about the track record of prior investments. This isn't as easy as asking a public stock mutual fund manager about their history, however. A private equity fund manager may be reluctant to share their track record of performance for several reasons.

- One primary concern is confidentiality and competitive advantage. Sharing detailed performance data could reveal proprietary investment strategies, deal flow, or other sensitive information the manager prefers to keep private to maintain a competitive edge in the market.
- Often, a large part of the outperformance is that the GP has negotiated private favorable economics with the Sponsors they invest in. There are strict non-disclosure agreements (NDAs) surrounding these arrangements.
- Of course, if the fund's performance has been subpar or inconsistent, the manager may be hesitant to disclose this information to potential investors, as it could negatively impact fundraising efforts or reputation.
- Furthermore, regulatory restrictions or compliance concerns may limit the manager's ability to share performance data, particularly if it includes sensitive financial information or conflicts with securities laws.

Overall, the decision to share track records of performance is complex and may involve weighing confidentiality, competitiveness, regulatory compliance, and investor relations considerations. Don't be surprised if it's much more difficult to get track record information from some than you'd expect.

On request, Ironton is happy to discuss prior performance as part of a potential investor's due diligence process.

Other alternatives will likely also welcome the chance to discuss their track record and experience with you, and how it relates to your current decision.

## 5. Liquidity

When asking about investment liquidity and exit strategies, it's important to understand how easy it would be to convert your investment into cash if needed.

- Liquidity refers to how quickly and easily you can sell your stake in an investment and access your money.
- Real estate investments are typically MUCH less liquid than stocks or bonds, as selling a property can take time and may be subject to market conditions.
- Inquire about potential exit strategies, such as selling the property, refinancing, or participating in a buyout agreement.

Understanding these options allows you to plan for potential financial needs or changes in circumstances and ensures that your investment remains flexible and aligned with your overall financial strategy.

Ask the Sponsor or GP about the liquidity options, if any, for the investment you are considering. Many passive real estate investments will require 4-6 years of commitment with no liquidity. This is what you give up earning up to twice the return you would get in the stock market!

## 6. Due Diligence

Inquiring about the due diligence process is crucial before investing in real estate.

- Thoroughly evaluate the property and its management procedures to ensure it meets your investment criteria.
- Property evaluations assess factors like location, condition, and potential for rental income or appreciation.

- Understanding the management procedures involves knowing how the property will be operated and maintained, including tenant management, maintenance schedules, and financial reporting.
- Understand how these aspects will be handled and what safeguards are in place to protect your investment.

Conducting thorough due diligence helps mitigate risks and ensures the investment aligns with your financial goals and expectations.

If you pursue the Syndication option, you will select projects and their Sponsors directly. This is like selecting a portfolio of individual stocks based on your own research. In this case, you will have considerable research to do here.

If you pursue the Private Equity fund option, you just need to trust the General Partners of the fund and their strategy. You are then delegating to the GP to research each individual Sponsor and project. This is like investing in a mutual fund to save yourself the headache of research.

## 7. Hold Title

Talk to your attorney and CPA; they can guide you through this process. For example, you can hold the investment in your name or jointly with your spouse. You may discover, through estate planning, it makes sense to develop a trust to hold these investments. These are just some possibilities. Your attorney, CPA, or financial planner may have other suggestions.

Ask the GP in the Fund if you are allowed to change how you hold title if your estate planning needs evolve over time. Most should offer flexibility to change how you hold title, and most General Partners should have the ability.

### 8. Fund the Investment

If you are investing with cash, this is as simple as wiring the funds to the General Partner.

If you are using a self-directed IRA, you may need to have a self-directed custodian that supports working with real estate investments. Most do not! You can ask the GP of your fund, or your CPA, for recommendations.

Be aware that moving funds from your traditional IRA (such as Schwab, Fidelity, or Vanguard) to your self-directed custodian could take a few weeks. Once your funds are transferred, the new custodian might require a week (or more) to make the investment, once you provide the "Direction of Investment" paperwork. As you are interviewing different service providers, ask them about this. Usually they can move faster, but they may charge expedite fees to do so.

## Closing Thoughts

Real estate investment is our passion. Every day, Lon still dives into active and passive investing, but not everyone has the time or passion for real estate that he does. He strongly believes that everyone should have access to this vehicle for growing their financial freedom.

You have now learned what we consider to be the most essential elements to passive investing while closely managing your risk. Now it's time for you to take the next step and get started talking to your family and advisors. Decide on where you want to go, your risk tolerance to get there, and then plan the vehicles for wealth that are right for you.

And if Ironton Capital can be of service to you for your journey, then reach out to us at https://irontoncapital.com/gopassive and let's talk about how our passive funds could fit into your portfolio.

# Chapter 12: Implement

We've spent the previous chapters exploring strategy, options, and frameworks. Now it's time to talk execution—the practical, step-by-step mechanics of completing a 1031 exchange (or evaluating whether a taxable sale makes more sense).

This is where theory meets reality. We've seen investors who understood every basic conceptual aspect of 1031 exchanges still stumble on execution. They miss deadlines by a day. They inadvertently trigger constructive receipt. They identify the wrong properties or work with the wrong professionals. The difference between a successful tax deferral and an unexpected tax bill often comes down to precision in implementation.

This chapter is your field manual.

We'll walk through the entire process chronologically, identify the critical decision points, build in contingencies for when things go wrong (because they often do), and share the hard-won lessons from tens of thousands of exchanges.

## Phase 1: Pre-Exchange Planning

We have found that investors who invest time in pre-exchange planning—in conjunction with a good QI—execute dramatically smoother 1031s.

### Step 1: Confirm Your Investment Intent

The IRS requires that both your relinquished property and replacement property be held "*for productive use in a trade or business or for investment.*"

**What We Look For:**

- **Holding Period:** While there's no bright-line rule, we generally recommend at least a 12-24 month holding period before exchange. If you're coming off a short hold (under a year), try to document your long-term investment intent (operating statements, maintenance records, tenant leases, management agreements).
- **Rental Activity:** For properties with any personal use component like a vacation home, verify compliance with Revenue Procedure 2008-16. The pattern is specific: rent the dwelling for at least 14 days in each of previous two 12-month periods, while limiting personal use to the greater of 14 days or 10% of the days rented in each period.
- **Business Purpose:** Document the business rationale for the property. If audited years later, you need to demonstrate this wasn't held primarily for sale.

**Red Flags We Watch For:**

- Properties purchased, renovated, and quickly flipped
- Properties with excessive personal use relative to rental activity

**Pro Tip:** Properties acquired specifically to facilitate another 1031 exchange automatically qualify. Strange but true. One of our clients traded into a property and about three months later a hospital came knocking on his door and said they wanted to buy it. The client turned around and immediately did another 1031 exchange just down the road to another building. Zero concern about 1031 eligibility because of the client's intent to 1031 into another long-term investment property.

## Step 2: Resolve Entity and Title Issues

The "same taxpayer rule" requires that the entity selling the relinquished property must be the same entity acquiring the replacement property. This is where partnership structures, LLCs, and trusts create complexity.

**Partnership Considerations:** If your property is held in a partnership or multi-member LLC, and partners have different goals (some want cash, others want to exchange), you must resolve this *before* listing. We've seen this destroy many, many potential 1031s when discovered too late.

The full scope of partnership issues and solutions is beyond the scope of this book. This is one of the most common 1031 complications as well as one of the most legally dense and unsettled given all the potential permutations.

## Step 3: Select and Engage Your Qualified Intermediary

Your QI selection is critical. Your 1031 intermediary is your guide through a complex and unintuitive web of state and federal rules. This entity will control your entire sales proceeds—potentially millions of dollars—for up to 180 days.

### QI Selection Criteria

- **Experience:** Even very smart people need years of seasoning to competently navigate the 1031 space. Bias toward teams with different forms of deep experience (attorneys, accountants, former brokers, former financial advisors, etc.).
- **Financial Security:** Look for segregated qualified escrow or trust accounts (your funds never commingle with their operating funds or other clients' money), fidelity bonds and errors & omissions insurance, annual audited financials

- **<u>Professional Credentials</u>:** While not legally required, Certified Exchange Specialist (CES®) designation and Federation of Exchange Accommodators (FEA) membership indicate commitment to ongoing education and industry best practices.
- **<u>Geographic Experience</u>:** Familiarity with your state's specific requirements and local title company practices should be a consideration.
- **<u>Technology and Security</u>:** Secure document portals, battle-tested wire fraud prevention procedures, cyber liability insurance, and speed of processing are critical.
- **<u>Fee Transparency</u>:** There should be a clear fee structure (typically $800-$1,500 for standard exchanges).

### Critical Questions to Ask

- "How are exchange funds secured and what insurance coverage do you carry?"
- "Walk me through your wire verification procedures—how do you prevent fraud?"
- "What's your procedure if I cannot complete my exchange?"
- "Can you provide references from recent clients with similar transaction sizes?"

## <u>Optional Step 4</u>: Prepare Your Purchase and Sale Agreement

The property purchase agreement for your sale can (but does not necessarily need to) include specific 1031 exchange language. While customary, we do not actively recommend this.

First, let's cover what this looks like and then we'll explain why we dislike it.

## Sample Contract Provision

"Seller intends to complete a 1031 tax-deferred exchange and reserves the right to assign this contract to a Qualified Intermediary. Buyer agrees to cooperate with such assignment and acknowledges that this cooperation creates no additional liability or cost to Buyer."

**What This Accomplishes:**

- Notifies the buyer you're exchanging (eliminates surprises at closing)
- Permits assignment to the QI
- Protects you from buyer objections or renegotiation based on the exchange

The exchange doesn't fail for lack of magic contract words if assignments and notices are otherwise properly executed. There is a legal requirement that the counterparty (buyer) knows about your 1031 exchange before the deed transfers; however, this can take place at any time—even at the closing table.

**Why We Don't Like Cooperation Clauses**

1031s are unfortunately not very widely understood. Such clauses are just as apt to create more confusion or uncertainty for the buyer (or their agent) as they are to demonstrate seriousness or clarity. An inexperienced buyer might become worried about complexity or delays, especially when cooperation clauses are written into offer letters (as sometimes happens). On the flip side, savvy and experienced sellers (when you are buying your next property) might understand that you have valuation and timeline concerns and use this as negotiating leverage against you.

To prevent these issues, our company issues 1031 notices to all parties at closing that effectively state *"Our client is performing a 1031 exchange. This does not affect you as the buyer/seller. Please sign here saying you understand this."*

## Step 5: Begin Identifying Potential Replacement Properties

Don't wait until after your sale closes. Start identifying potential replacement properties during the listing period.

If you close your relinquished property with 2-3 replacement properties already identified and under contract (subject to your exchange timeline), you've compressed your risk dramatically.

This preparation doesn't commit you to anything, but it accelerates execution once the clock starts.

# Phase 2: Exchange Execution (Days 0-45)

Remember, the IRS time periods are absolute. The 45-Day Identification Period starts the day after you close on your sale and the identification must be in writing, signed, and delivered to your QI. See Chapter 1 for more details.

# Phase 3: Closing the Replacement Property

## The Reverse Flow of Funds

At closing, the process reverses. Like the sale of the relinquished property, title typically passes directly between parties rather than through the QI:

1. The QI is assigned into the replacement property purchase contract.
2. The QI uses exchange proceeds to fund the purchase.
3. Title deeds directly from the seller to you.
4. The QI maintains control through contractual assignments and notices.
5. The exchange is complete.

## Critical Requirements

- You must receive "substantially the same property" you identified on day 45.
- Any improvements or construction must be completed and paid for before you take receipt (under Revenue Procedures 2000-37 and 2004-51, improvement exchanges use an Exchange Accommodation Titleholder structure).
- The same taxpayer acquiring property must match the owner of entity that sold.

## What Qualifies as Real Property

Since the Tax Cuts and Jobs Act of 2017, only real property qualifies for 1031 treatment. Personal property exchanges were eliminated. However, "incidental personal property" received with real property (furniture, fixtures, equipment) doesn't blow the exchange. The regulations provide a 15% aggregate fair market value test: if the incidental personal property doesn't exceed 15% of the total property value, it's still treated as boot but doesn't disqualify the exchange.

## Dealing with Boot

If you cannot reinvest all proceeds or trade down in value, you'll receive boot—taxable gain up to the amount of boot received. (Recall the material covered in Chapter 9.)

**Example of Cash Boot:**

- Relinquished property: $3 million
- Replacement property: $2.7 million
- Proceeds not reinvested: $300,000 (taxable boot)

**Example of Mortgage Boot:**

- Relinquished property: $2 million value, $800,000 mortgage
- Replacement property: $2.2 million value, $600,000 mortgage
- Net mortgage relief: $200,000 (taxable mortgage boot)

The $200,000 mortgage relief is treated as cash received. To the extent you have gain in the property, this will trigger recognized gain. Depreciation recapture on that boot is generally taxed at up to 25%, while remaining gain receives long-term capital gains treatment.

**How to Avoid Mortgage Boot:**

Add cash equity to replace the debt reduction. In the example above, adding $200,000 of your own cash to the replacement property purchase eliminates the mortgage boot.

**Post-closing Cash Flow Strategy:**

If your goal is to access cash, you don't have to take it as boot. Complete the exchange fully, then refinance the replacement property 2-

3 months later. Cash-out refinance proceeds are non-taxable because they're loan proceeds you must repay (not classified as income).

### Post-Exchange Documentation

After closing, you're responsible for filing Form 8824 (Like-Kind Exchanges) with your tax return for the year of the exchange. Complete it using the closing statements and exchange documentation the QI provides. This form reports the exchange details, calculates your deferred gain, and establishes the basis in your replacement property.

## Contingency Planning—When Things Go Wrong

Even with perfect planning, exchanges face challenges. Here's how we handle the most common failure points.

### Contingency 1: Your Property Sale Delayed; Your Purchase Is Going to Happen First

**The Problem:**

Your property isn't selling, your buyer backs out, or closing delays push you past your replacement property's availability.

**Solutions:**

- **Extend replacement property closing:** Negotiate extensions with the seller if possible.
- **Bridge financing, then Reverse 1031:** Use short-term financing to secure the replacement property, then complete a reverse exchange.

**Reverse Exchange Mechanics:**

Please see Chapter 9 for a detailed description on Reverse 1031 Exchanges.

## Contingency 2: Identified Property Falls Through After Day 45

**The Problem:**

Your identified replacement property fails during due diligence, or the seller backs out. You cannot re-identify after day 45.

**Solutions:**

- **If you identified multiple properties:** Pivot immediately to your backup properties.
- **If you identified only one property:** You're potentially facing a failed exchange.

**Prevention:**

It's often, but not always, a good idea to identify 2-3 properties using the three-property rule. This gives you backup options. DSTs are a popular backup option.

## Contingency 3: Cash Flow or Emergency Needs

**The Problem:**

You need cash during the exchange period due to emergency or unexpected expenses.

**The Hard Truth:**

You cannot access exchange funds without disqualifying the exchange. There's no emergency exception. You cannot pledge the exchange proceeds as collateral against a loan. Any QI promising to return funds to you early is putting you at significant audit risk.

**The 46th-day Exception:**

If you decide that you need cash and do not want to complete your 1031 exchange AND it is before your 45-day ID period ends, you can do the following:

1. Tell your QI to wipe your 45-day ID list clean (no properties identified).
2. Wait until the 45-day period ends.
3. At Day 46, with no properties ID'd, the potential for a valid 1031 exchange is now over. Therefore, your QI can release your escrowed sale proceeds to you without creating audit risk.

**Options:**

- **Personal credit:** Use personal credit lines, home equity, or other resources.
- **Post-exchange refinance:** If you can wait until after closing the replacement property, refinance immediately.

## Contingency 4: Unable to Find Suitable Replacement Property

**The Problem:**

You searched diligently but nothing meets your criteria by day 45.

**Options:**

- **Identify properties anyway:** Choose the "least worst" options and hope market conditions improve.
- **Accept failed exchange:** Take the tax hit this year and potentially reinvest in a taxable transaction.
- **"Parking Lot" strategy:** This is our own term. You can use a 1031 exchange as a financial parking lot—something to pull into and then back out of again. Identify a stable asset to trade into, complete your 1031 exchange, and then continue looking for a more suitable long-term property. Once you find this, complete another 1031 exchange out of your "parking lot" investment and into the better long-term fit.

Sometimes the best exchange is no exchange. There are ways to attempt to offset even very large tax bills; these are rarely as smooth as a 1031 exchange, but the options exist.

# Implementation Checklist: Your Exchange Execution Map

Exchanges can involve many steps, making it easy to miss something. A checklist helps ensure nothing gets missed and your exchange stays compliant. You'll find a great one in Chapter 1.

# Advanced Execution Scenarios

## Multiple Property Exchanges

Exchanging multiple relinquished properties for multiple replacement properties adds complexity but follows the same core principles.

**<u>The Challenge</u>:**

Matching proceeds from multiple closings (potentially on different dates) with multiple replacement property acquisitions while staying within the 45/180-day windows.

**<u>The Strategy</u>:**

1. Treat the earliest closing as Day 0 for the entire exchange if running one consolidated exchange.
2. Alternatively, structure separate exchange agreements for each relinquished property to create independent timelines (when facts permit).
3. Identify replacement properties by 45 days from Day 0 (or respective closing dates if separate exchanges).
4. Complete all acquisitions within 180 days of respective starting dates.
5. Allocate proceeds and basis across replacement properties proportionally

**<u>Example</u>:**

You sell Property A (closes March 1) and Property B (closes March 15). If running one consolidated exchange, your 45-day identification period begins March 1 (expires April 15). Your 180-day period also begins March 1 (expires August 28). You can identify multiple replacement properties totaling the combined value of A and B.

## Build-to-Suit / Improvement Exchanges

If you want to use exchange proceeds to construct improvements on a replacement property, special rules apply under Revenue Procedures 2000-37 and 2004-51.

**The Core Limitation**

You must receive the completed improved property. Only improvements that are completed and paid for before you take title count toward the exchange value. Construction time counts against your 180-day deadline.

**The Practical Reality**

You typically have 135 days maximum for construction (180 days minus 45-day identification period). Complex construction projects rarely complete in this timeframe.

**Potential Danger**

As previously mentioned, only improvements which are completed and invoiced before you take title count toward your exchange value. If you take title to a partially completed project, the incomplete improvements don't count, potentially creating a shortfall.

# When to Consider Abandoning the Exchange

Sometimes the best decision is to pay the tax and walk away. We've seen investors make questionable investment decisions just to avoid current tax liability; however, 1031 QIs are prohibited from offering direct investment advice.

**Consider a Taxable Sale When:**

- You can't find suitable investment properties within your criteria.
- Your gain is minimal and tax cost is manageable.
- You're facing personal liquidity needs that cannot wait.
- You're in an unusually low tax year (temporary income reduction).
- Alternative investments (private placements, REITs, business opportunities, stock market) seem likely to outperform 1031-eligible options.

**The Psychological Trap**

Investors can become fixated on tax deferral and lose sight of investment quality. Remember: a 1031 exchange is a tool to facilitate good investments, not a requirement to make bad ones.

## Closing Thoughts

The 1031 exchange isn't your only option. See the other chapters of this book to help identify alternatives for your unique situation. Chapter 8 shows a financial model for the impact of different strategies.

For 1031 exchange guidance, visit https://1031x.com

For more info on passive investing with fund of funds, reach out to us at http://irontoncapital.com/gopassive to learn more about our funds and to see if they are a great fit for your portfolio.

# Chapter 13: Decision Framework

Have you ever sat down to plan your financial future and wondered:

- Will I have enough for retirement?
- Can I retire comfortably before I'm too old to enjoy it?
- Will I be able to… send a child or grandchild to college, own a family vacation home, leave a legacy for my family, or give back to my community?

Then you pulled out your computer and checked out Oppenheimer, Fidelity, Vanguard or a similar web site. You were probably told that your current rate of savings, combined with typical stock market returns, will not enable you to meet your goals. You need to find another way.

Retirement worries are common among Americans, with a notable percentage expressing concerns about their financial readiness for later years. The Employee Benefit Research Institute's 2021 survey revealed that 4 in 10 American workers are projected to fall short of what they need in retirement savings. This finding underscores the widespread nature of retirement anxieties, cutting across various demographics.

The Pew Research Center's study highlighted the generational aspect of these concerns, with 61% of young adults, 64% of middle-aged adults, and 57% of older adults expressing worry about their retirement savings.

You've likely discovered that real estate is likely part of the solution to your financial objectives. It will diversify your investments from just stocks and bonds and historically it generates much higher returns.

But you are likely a busy professional, with an even busier partner. Whatever limited free time you do have, you don't want to spend running real estate investments. Isn't there a way to invest passively with a managed amount of risk?

That's what we're here to investigate together in this Chapter.

## Retirement Calculator – Stocks/Bonds Plan

Briefly, let's determine how much you can withdraw from your retirement savings annually while ensuring it lasts your lifetime. This depends on various factors, including your age, life expectancy, investment returns, and spending habits. You'll want to work with your CPA or financial planner to develop a more robust estimate than the quick estimate here, but this should give you a rough idea.

A common rule of thumb is the 4% rule, which suggests withdrawing 4% of your retirement savings in the first year and adjusting for inflation thereafter.

For example, if you have $500,000 saved, you could withdraw $20,000 in the first year. This rule aims to balance spending needs with the preservation of savings.

In other words, to get $1 of consistent retirement income, you need $25 in savings. The formula is:

**$1 spending / 4% return = $25 in savings**

If you want $200,000 of annual income in retirement:

**$200,000 annual spend / 4% return = $5,000,000 in savings**

No wonder so many people are stressed about retirement savings!

Vanguard reports that over the last 70 years, a typical 60% stock and 40% bond portfolio has generated an average annual return of approximately 7% to 8%. Actual returns can vary depending on specific market conditions and investment strategies employed within the portfolio.

(For more see:
https://corporate.vanguard.com/content/corporatesite/us/en/corp/articles/global-60-40-portfolio-steady-as-it-goes.html?)

And over the past 70 years, the average US rate of inflation has been about 3% per year. This figure reflects the general increase in prices for goods and services over an extended period, as measured by indices such as the Consumer Price Index (CPI).

The 4% withdraw rule is just the expected return (7%) less the expected inflation (3%). The amount you can draw out of savings each year will grow a bit, to keep pace with inflation.

**7% total return – 3% expected inflation =**
**4% annual withdraw amount**

## Retirement Calculator – Real Estate Plan

If you want a better retirement lifestyle, you need to increase the return from 7-8% to something higher, without taking a lot of extra risk – and that's why a lot of us turn to real estate.

A well-diversified real portfolio of 30-40 commercial properties can generate a return of 17-20% per year. Assume 17% and take 3% off for the inflation factor. That leaves 14%.

How does this impact your savings requirement?

**$200,000 annual spend / 14% return = $1,430,000 in savings**

You have reduced your savings requirement from $5,000,000 to $1,430,000 and still achieved the same $200,000 annual spend goal.

And there are advantages to being risk adverse. A well-diversified real estate portfolio typically exhibits lower investment return risk compared to a stock and bond portfolio.

As an asset class, real estate also benefits from unique tax advantages—including depreciation (including bonus depreciation), operational deductions, and the ability to 1031 exchange upon sale. Real estate returns are notably less volatile than the average annual return of U.S. stocks, as reported by data from the Credit Suisse Global Investment Returns Yearbook. While real estate values can fluctuate, they generally don't experience the same level of short-term price swings as stocks.

In fact, according to research by the National Council of Real Estate Investment Fiduciaries (NCREIF), real estate investments often provide more stable and predictable returns over the long term, with less volatility than stocks.

What's the drawback? Liquidity.

It's essential to note that **real estate investments are much less liquid than stocks and bonds**, meaning they can be harder to sell quickly if needed. (This is particularly true for DSTs.) You wouldn't want *all* your portfolio to be in real estate for this reason. You've got to be diversified.

## Retirement Calculator – Diversified Plan

Overall, a diversified portfolio including both real estate and stocks/bonds can help mitigate overall investment risk while potentially enhancing returns.

For example, if you put half of your savings into diversified real estate and half into a traditional stock/bond portfolio, you'd expect a return about halfway between 7-8% (stocks/bonds) and 17-20% (real estate), or 13%. Take out 3% for inflation. How much savings do we need now?

**$200,000 annual spend / 10% return = $2,000,000 in savings**

For most Americans, saving $2,000,000 for retirement is a lot more realistic than saving $5,000,000. You can retire sooner and retire better by adding real estate for diversification.

## Active or Passive Real Estate?

Now that you understand that you need some real estate in your portfolio, should you invest in active or passive real estate?

You may have had a life-long dream to own and/or operate a real estate investment. If that is the case, you should follow your passion! If on the other hand investing is just a means to an end, this book hopefully gives you a lot of options.

## Understanding Correlation

We often talk about how investors build portfolios. One of the key ideas behind smart portfolios is correlation — how different investments move in relation to one another.

Correlation is a number that shows how two things move together. If one thing goes up and the other usually goes up too, the correlation is close to +1.0 (Figure 13-1).

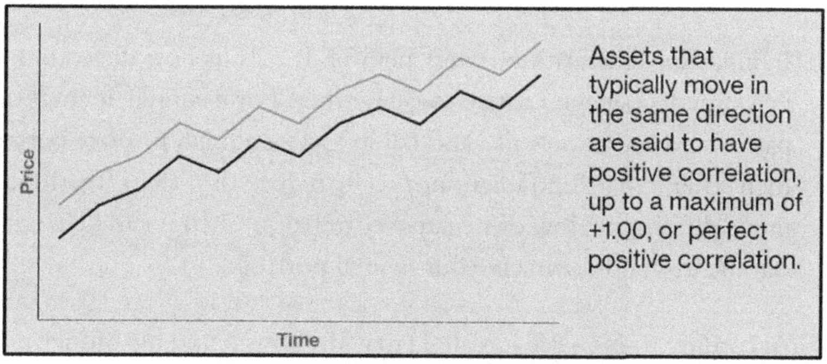


**Figure 13-1: Example Correlation of +1.0**

If Investment A rises by 10% and Investment B almost always rises by 10% too, then their correlation might be **+0.90** (very high). That means when A goes up, B goes up almost the same amount; when A falls, B falls too.

If one thing goes up and the other usually goes down, the correlation is close to -1.0 (Figure 13-2).

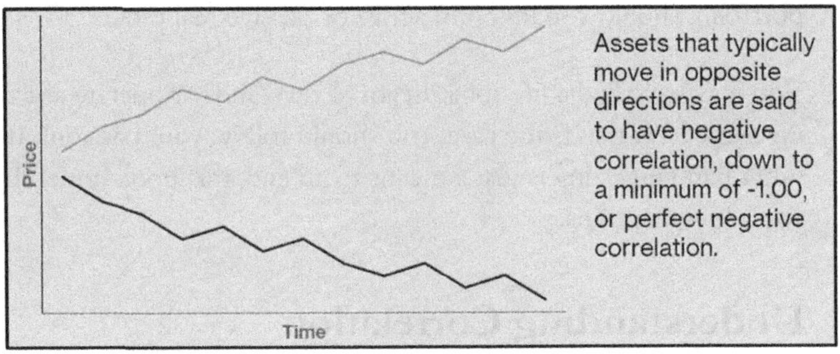


**Figure 13-2: Example Correlation of -1.0**

If they move with no reliable pattern, the correlation is near 0.

Now imagine Investment C instead. When Investment A rises by 10%, Investment C stays flat or rises only slightly; when A falls, C may still rise or at least fall much less. Their correlation might be **+0.10** or near **0** (very low). That means A and C don't move together much.

In investing, correlation is very helpful. It tells us how different kinds of investments behave relative to each other. For example, if stocks and a particular fund always rise and fall in lockstep (high positive correlation), then adding that fund might not really reduce risk. But if the funds move differently (low or negative correlation) then it can help smooth out the ups and downs in your overall portfolio.

According to Nobel Laureate Harry Markowitz and his Modern Portfolio Theory, two assets that move together add less diversification benefit than two assets that don't.

When we add an investment that has low or no correlation with stocks and bonds, our overall risk often goes down without sacrificing return. Or in some cases, the return goes up while risk stays the same. That's a powerful idea.

In simple terms:

- If you put all your money into investments that behave very similarly, a drop in one will likely hit all.
- If you include investments that behave differently, you build a buffer for your portfolio.

When the team at Ironton looks at our income fund strategies, we explicitly target assets that are not highly correlated to standard stocks or bonds. That way, when stock markets wobble, our positions have the potential to hold firm (or even move differently).

Now let's turn to Ironton's Medium-Term Income (MTI) Fund and how it performs in real-world terms. We believe the MTI Fund stands out because:

- It outperforms typical stock and bond allocations over time.
- It is not highly correlated with either the stock market or traditional bond markets.
- It adds diversification and stability to the overall portfolio.

When many investors compare stocks and bonds, they often assume these two asset types will cover most of the risk-return tradeoff. But markets change. Bonds may suffer when interest rates rise. Stocks may decline in recessions. In contrast, the MTI Fund is structured to generate steady income and moderate growth, using assets that behave differently than these two conventional legs.

Because of this different behavior, the MTI Fund has the potential to deliver strong returns and reduce overall portfolio volatility. In practical terms, when stocks are flat or falling, the MTI fund has shown resilience. When bonds face headwinds, the MTI still generates income. And when both stocks and bonds rally, the effect of the MTI is additive rather than duplicative.

Reach out to us at http://irontoncapital.com/gopassive to learn more about this fund to see if it is a fit for your portfolio.

## Common Mistakes

Here is a summary of common problems many people experience when planning their investment portfolio.

- Jumping between asset classes to try to time the market
- Overconcentrating in a single asset class
- Not diversifying across geographies, strategy, sectors, vintages, asset life cycles, etc.
- Not having a clear overall investment strategy
- Making investments because you can, not because they are the right investment
- Under-allocating to private asset classes

Figure 13-3 outlines potential solutions to some of these common mistakes.

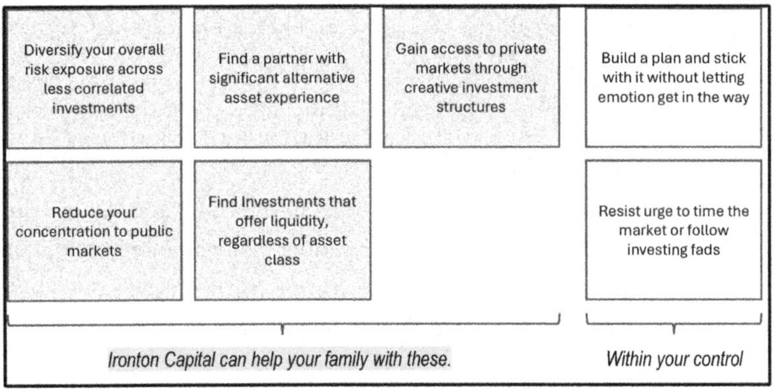


**Figure 13-3: Solutions to Common Mistakes**

## What to Do Now

Many of our readers are professionals that have invested in years of education and work to master their field. Real estate investing is its own specialty and requires the same care and time to build expertise for profitable returns. Often, building that expertise creates another part- to full-time job that they just do not have time for. That's why many have discovered passive investing. They've hired an expert to handle the details so they can instead focus on their lives and families and retire on their own timetable.

If you **have enough money** to achieve your financial goals, you might want to:

- Select investments in generally lower risk categories
- Increase your diversification to reduce risk
- Move from active to passive to gain more free time

If on the other hand you **have not yet saved enough** to meet your targets, you can work with a financial planner to develop a forecast for your future with your current portfolio.

If the current plan shows you are very likely to be on track to meet your financial goals in the future, you can either:

- Keep doing what you are doing and accept the target retirement date.
- Evaluate some of the options in the book and see if a different mix of investments might reduce risk while increasing returns. This might enable you to either retire with the same income at an earlier date, or to keep your current retirement date and exit with more money.

We see that most younger investors with jobs are more risk tolerant. They have plenty of time to let compounding do its magic to help them reach their goals. If they have the time, skill and desire, these tend to be active real estate investors as well. As investors get older, get tired of fighting the battles of the active real estate investors, and/or get close to (or exceed) their financial target, they tend to shift to more passive and conservative strategies.

We also tend to see that younger investors often have great current incomes, so they build portfolios that are long term growth focused – there isn't a need for current income. As we work with more mature investors, the mix from long term appreciation to predictable, current cash flow tends to become a bigger consideration.

We wrote this book to give you the framework. But frameworks only go so far. Your situation has its own numbers, its own deadlines, and its own complexities. When you're ready to get specific, the 1031X team is here. Reach us at 1-888-899-1031 or visit you're your time at https://1031x.com/free-consultation

Or to brainstorm how the ideas in this book can fit into your passive investing goals, head to http://irontoncapital.com/gopassive to book a time with us at Ironton Capital.

Thanks for taking the time to read it with us!

# Appendix A: 1031 Exchange FAQ

A 1031 exchange is not just a tax strategy; it's a precision exercise in timing, documentation, and intent. The most successful investors treat it as part of their capital-allocation discipline—an important tool in their real estate toolkit.

## What is a 1031 exchange?

A 1031 exchange lets you sell one investment property and reinvest the proceeds into another qualified property, deferring capital gains and depreciation-recapture taxes (among others).

## What exactly does Section 1031 allow?

Section 1031 of the Internal Revenue Code allows investors to sell one property held for business or investment use and reinvest the proceeds into another property of "like kind." When executed properly, this exchange defers taxes normally due in the year of sale. The law doesn't eliminate taxes; it repositions capital without interrupting its compounding potential.

## What qualifies as "like-kind" real estate?

For tax purposes, like-kind refers to the nature of the investment, not its grade or asset class. Any U.S. real property held for business or investment use generally qualifies. A multifamily property can exchange into industrial, hospitality into retail, raw land into net-leased assets. The intent must remain investment-oriented; personal residences, flips, and inventory do not qualify.

## Who is required to handle the exchange?

In almost all cases, a Qualified Intermediary (QI) must hold proceeds from the sale to preserve tax deferral. The QI structures the documentation, maintains escrow, and promotes compliance with IRS timelines and language.

## How does the process work in practice?

1. Sell your relinquished property. Proceeds go directly to the QI, not to you.
2. Identify potential replacement properties within 45 calendar days of closing.
3. Acquire one or more of those identified properties within 180 days.

There are many more potential rules and structure, but this is the basic procedure.

## What deadlines matter most?

The IRS imposes two hard-stops:

- **45-Day Identification Period** – You must submit a written list of potential replacements to your QI.
- **180-Day Exchange Period** – You must close on one or more of those identified assets.

No extensions are granted except in federally declared disaster areas.

## How is "boot" defined and taxed?

"Boot" is any value received that isn't like-kind property—cash, personal property, debt relief not offset by new debt, etc. Boot is taxable to the extent of recognized gain.

## Can I defer all taxes from sale?

Yes—if the replacement property equals or exceeds the relinquished property's net sales price and you reinvest all net equity.

## What are the different types of 1031 exchanges?

- **Forward Exchange:** The standard model—sell first, buy second.
- **Reverse Exchange:** Acquire the replacement before selling; often used when desirable inventory is scarce.
- **Improvement/Build-to-Suit Exchange:** Use exchange funds for construction or capital improvements before taking title. Each requires precise structuring, separate entities, and compliance with Rev. Proc. 2000-37 and subsequent guidance.

## Can multiple properties be involved?

Yes. The code permits one-to-many, many-to-one, or many-to-many exchanges. Aggregating or diversifying is allowed so long as identification and closing timelines are met.

## Can exchange proceeds fund closing costs or fees?

Only certain transactional costs—broker commissions, title insurance, escrow fees—qualify. Costs related to financing, prorations, repairs, or due diligence do not and will generate taxable boot if paid from exchange funds.

## How are proceeds held during the exchange?

Proceeds should be held in segregated, FDIC-insured accounts controlled solely by the Qualified Intermediary in a Qualified Escrow or Qualified Trust account. At 1031X, for example, each client's funds are assigned a unique account under their taxpayer identification number. No funds are commingled or invested.

## How long must I hold the new property before another exchange?

The tax code doesn't specify a minimum, but intent governs. Twelve months is a reasonable and common rule of thumb, but there are exceptions.

## Can I perform successive exchanges indefinitely?

Yes. There's no statutory limit. Many investors employ a "swap 'til you drop" strategy—continuously exchanging and stepping up basis at death, thereby eliminating deferred gains for heirs. Estate and income tax planning should always be coordinated with counsel.

## Can partnerships, funds, or syndications execute 1031 exchanges?

Yes, though the structure matters. A partnership itself can exchange, but individual partners (LPs, for example) cannot exchange their interests independently. Some private funds may be structure to accommodate 1031 capital Tenancy-in-Common (TIC) "sidecars" or through DST restructuring.

## How do Delaware Statutory Trusts fit in?

A DST allows fractional ownership of institutional-grade assets while remaining eligible for 1031 exchange treatment. Sponsors typically acquire and manage stabilized assets—multifamily, industrial, medical office, etc.

## Can Private Equity sponsors use 1031 capital?

Historically, exchange funds were excluded from private equity structures due to partnership-interest prohibitions. New models now bridge this gap through Tenancy-in-Common structures, DST conversions, or hybrid master-escrow agreements.

## What does a typical 1031 exchange cost?

Fees vary by complexity. For most institutional-level standard exchanges, fees range between $800 and $1,500 per relinquished property. For portfolios or recurring transactions, enterprise pricing can be arranged.

## What happens if I miss a deadline or identification rule?

Failure to identify or close within the statutory windows disqualifies the exchange, and the deferred gain becomes immediately taxable. The IRS provides no "good-faith" exceptions.

## Can a 1031 intermediary help with my tax return?

No. A QI can explain mechanics but cannot advise on tax positions, entity structure, or perform basis calculations. (The same goes for formal legal or financial advice).

## Where can I learn more or connect with a pro?

Educational resources, technical briefs, and real-time consultations are available at 1031x.com. Investors managing recurring dispositions or fund-level transactions can request a confidential strategy review directly through the firm's institutional team. For 1031 exchange guidance, visit https://1031x.com

# Appendix B: Optimize Your IRA

What if you have a rollover 401K from an old employer, and/or a self-directed IRA? It's probably invested in the stock and bond market now, getting (historically) a return of around 7-8% per year.

If you move it to a self-directed IRA custodian, your menu of investing choices will be much broader than the mutual funds you likely have available to you now. For example, you could invest in an Ironton long term fund like the National Diversified Fund (NDF).

One interesting approach is to invest in NDF or a similar private equity fund that is illiquid (e.g., you cannot sell shares in a market like you can a mutual fund), and comes with no decision rights. You can then engage a specialized CPA to do a Fair Market Value (FMV) assessment of your investment. In most cases, because the investment is not liquid and doesn't give you decision rights, the FMV could be less than the original amount of your investment.

You can give the CPA's FMV analysis to your IRA custodian, and they will reduce the market value (on paper – in reality, the value does not change, of course) of your IRA as a result.

From there, you can then convert your traditional IRA to a Roth IRA. You will, of course, owe the taxes on the value at the time of the conversion, but that cost is much lower since the FMV has lowered the value. As with any other Roth IRA, it will now grow tax free. The after-tax savings can be considerable.

To see this more in-depth, get our free training on How to Optimize Your IRA for a Big Tax savings at https://irontoncapital.com/bigirasavings and then talk to your CPA to see if this tax strategy is right for you.

# Appendix C:
# July 2025 Tax Law at a Glance

The July 2025 tax law introduced major changes that have a meaningful impact on real estate investors:

- Opportunity Zone (OZ) Program Overhaul
- Reinstatement of 100% Bonus Depreciation
- Expanded Section 179 Rules

We'll also recap what didn't change and some thoughts on depreciation recapture.

## Opportunity Zone (OZ) Program Overhaul

The Opportunity Zone program, originally introduced as part of the 2017 Tax Cuts and Jobs Act, was made permanent but significantly restructured.

**Key Changes:**

- **Permanent Status**: The OZ program is no longer subject to renewal or sunset clauses.
- **Zone Redesignation**: A new set of qualifying zones has been designated for 2026 and beyond.
- **New 5-Year Step-Up**: Investors receive a 10% basis step-up after a 5-year hold (previously this benefit was 7 years, now simplified to 5).
- **Rural OZ Boost**: Qualified Rural Opportunity Funds (QROFs) offer a 30% step-up after 5 years, providing enhanced benefits to those targeting rural projects.

- **Stricter Compliance and Reporting**: Enhanced annual audit and community impact reporting requirements are now mandatory for all OZ funds.

**Implications for Investors:**

- Funds formed under the old rules must transition to the new compliance regime if they accept new capital.
- Investors with capital gains in 2025 should explore the redesigned OZs promptly to capture full benefits.
- Enhanced upside for rural-focused real estate strategies but… urban areas that were popular in the first release of the OZ have a lot of new restrictions.

## 100% Bonus Depreciation Reinstated

This is arguably the most investor-friendly provision in the tax law.

**Key Features:**

- **Full Expensing**: Investors can once again write off 100% of eligible property improvements and personal property in the first year.
- **Applies to Cost Segregation Studies**: Accelerated depreciation is back in full force, enhancing after-tax returns.
- **No Phase-Out**: The scheduled phase-down that began in 2023 has been repealed.

**Implications for Investors:**

- Real estate professionals and passive investors alike can significantly reduce taxable income in the early years of ownership.

- Funds and syndications that perform detailed cost segregation studies can offer enhanced first-year tax benefits to LPs.
- Makes "pay the tax and reinvest" strategies more appealing by front-loading depreciation to offset gains.

This change enhances the attractiveness of many private placement offerings and DSTs. See Chapter 1 (1031x details), Chapter 5 (DST details), Chapter 6 (Private Placement details), and Chapter 7 (OZ, Opportunity Zones) for use cases and illustrations.

## Expanded Section 179 Rules

Section 179 expensing was enhanced alongside bonus depreciation—but real estate investors should be mindful of **state-level deviations**.

### Key Changes:

- **Higher Limits:** The federal cap was increased (e.g., from ~$1M to $1.5M), and more asset types qualify.
- **Real Property Eligibility:** Certain structural components (roofs, HVAC, fire systems) are now clearly eligible for immediate write-off under expanded definitions.
- **Partial Expensing of Large Projects:** Investors can combine Section 179 and bonus depreciation on the same asset for maximum impact.

### State-Level Nuance:

- Some states do **not** conform to federal Section 179 rules. Your deduction at the federal level may be added back on your state return.
- Here's a summary of **notable variances** by state (as of 2025 policy structures):

**Figure C-1: Variances to Federal Section 179**

Investor Impact:

- **Example Use Case:** A landlord replaces a roof and HVAC system at a 4-plex for $120K. Under OBBBA, the entire cost could be deductible in Year 1—federally—but not necessarily at the state level.
- Be sure to model the ***state-specific implications*** with your CPA, especially in high-income-tax states.

## What Didn't Change

Some key elements of the real estate tax code remained untouched:

- **1031 Exchanges**: Still available with no new limitations.
- **Capital Gains Tax Rates**: No increases were implemented.
- **Passive Activity Loss Rules**: No material changes.
- **SDIRA Real Estate Rules**: No new restrictions or penalties added.

## Depreciation Recapture: What You Must Understand

While strategies like cost segregation and bonus depreciation create substantial upfront tax savings, they come with a long-term tradeoff: **depreciation recapture**. The IRS will reclaim those deductions upon sale unless a 1031 exchange or other deferral mechanism is used.

- **More depreciation now = more recapture later**, unless you defer it.
- Tax rates differ:
  - **Capital gains** are taxed at **15–20%**, depending on income and asset type.
  - **Depreciation recapture** can be taxed up to **37%**, depending on whether it's categorized as unrecaptured §1250 gain or ordinary income (for personal property).

Section 1250 Property (real property like buildings/improvements) is taxed at 25% in most cases.

Section 1245 Property (equipment, furniture, appliances, etc.) can be cost segregated but recapture is at ordinary income rates (all the way up to 37%).

This is why exit planning and 1031 exchanges are so important: a well-timed exchange can defer not only capital gains, but also depreciation recapture—potentially for decades or permanently.

These continuities reinforce the value of real estate as a tax-efficient investment vehicle.

For 1031 exchange guidance, visit https://1031x.com

# Appendix D: Opportunity Zone Quick Overview

## Who Qualifies?

Any taxpayer with recognized capital gains (not ordinary income).

## What Qualifies?

Capital gains invested in a Qualified Opportunity Fund (QOF) within 180 days of realization.

## Investor Clocks:

- 180 days to invest gains in QOF
- Deferral of original gain until 12/31/2026 or earlier inclusion event
- 10-year hold for FMV step-up election (excludes QOF appreciation)

## QOF/QOZB Compliance Tests:

- **QOF**: 90% asset test (measured 2x/year), Form 8996 self-certification
- **QOZB**: Original use OR substantial improvement, 70% tangible property, working capital safe harbor (31 months), no NNN leases, no sin businesses

## Common Deal-Killers:

- Buying OZ property without QOF structure (no benefit)
- Missing 180-day reinvestment window

- Failing substantial improvement test (must double building basis)
- NNN lease structures (disqualified)
- Poor working capital documentation
- State non-conformity to federal OZ provisions

### When It Makes Sense:

- After taxable exit (1031 not available)
- 10+ year investment horizon
- Want to diversify beyond real property
- Confidence in sponsor's compliance capabilities
- State tax treatment is favorable or neutral

### When 1031 Is Better:

- Large low-basis real property
- Want full deferral (not just until 2026)
- Need depreciation benefits
- Shorter time horizon
- Want more control

For 1031 exchange guidance, visit https://1031x.com

# Appendix E: Glossary

**Accredited Investor** — An individual or entity that meets SEC income or net worth requirements, allowing investment in private placements and DSTs.

**Adjusted Basis** — The property's original purchase price plus improvements, minus depreciation. Used to calculate taxable gain.

**Amortization** — The process of gradually paying down loan principal through scheduled payments over time.

**Appreciation** — The increase in a property's market value over time.

**Asset Class** — A category of investment, such as multifamily, office, retail, industrial, or self-storage properties.

**Asset Manager/Sponsor** — Sources deals, secures financing, hires property managers, and guides the investment.

**Basis** — The owner's investment in a property for tax purposes, typically the purchase price plus acquisition costs.

**Boot** — Any cash, debt relief, or non-like-kind property received in a 1031 exchange. Boot is taxable.

**Capital Expenditures (CapEx)** — Money spent on improvements that extend the life or increase the value of a property (e.g., new roof, HVAC system).

**Capital Gains Tax** — Tax owed on the profit from selling an asset. For real estate, this includes both long-term capital gains and depreciation recapture.

**Cap Rate (Capitalization Rate)** — A common valuation metric: Net Operating Income ÷ Purchase Price. Used to compare investment yields across properties.

**Carried Interest** — A share of profits paid to a fund manager (GP) above their invested capital, often tax-advantaged if structured properly.

**Cash Balance Plan** — A type of defined-benefit retirement plan that allows large, tax-deferred contributions for business owners and high-income professionals.

**Cash Flow** — Net income from a property after expenses and debt service, usually measured monthly or annually.

**Cash on Cash** — Measures the annual return on the total cash invested; annual pre-tax cash flow ÷ total cash invested. Provides a snapshot of investment's current profitability.

**Concentration Risk** — Lack of diversification; Chance that amplified losses happen by relying too much on one asset or sector.

**Constructive Receipt** — An IRS doctrine where income is considered received (and taxable) even if the taxpayer hasn't physically taken possession. Avoided in 1031 exchanges by using a Qualified Intermediary.

**Cost Segregation Study** — An engineering study that reclassifies building components into shorter depreciation categories, accelerating tax deductions.

**Cross-Collateralization** — Using multiple properties as security for one loan, often in portfolio financing.

**Debt Service** — The total amount of principal and interest payments required on a loan.

**Debt Service Coverage Ratio (DSCR)** — A lender metric: Net Operating Income ÷ Annual Debt Service. A DSCR above 1.25 is often required.

**Deferral (Tax Deferral)** — Postponing taxes owed until a future date, often through a 1031 exchange or retirement account.

**Delaware Statutory Trust (DST)** — A legal structure allowing multiple investors to own fractional interests in real estate passively, commonly used for 1031 exchanges.

**Depreciation** — A tax deduction reflecting the gradual "wear and tear" of property improvements. Residential rental property is depreciated over 27.5 years; commercial over 39 years.

**Depreciation Recapture** — When selling, prior depreciation deductions are "recaptured" and taxed at a maximum federal rate of 25%.

**Diversification** — Spreading investments across asset classes, geographies, or sponsors to reduce risk.

**Due Diligence** — The investigation process before committing to an investment, including financial analysis, property inspections, sponsor background checks, and legal review.

**Equity Multiple** — A performance metric: Total Cash Returned ÷ Total Equity Invested.

**Exchange Accommodation Titleholder (EAT)** — Neutral third party that temporarily holds legal title so the taxpayer doesn't own both properties simultaneously, (allowing them to defer capital gains taxes while adhering to IRS rules).

**Exchange Period** — The 180-day window following the sale of a relinquished property during which the taxpayer must acquire replacement property.

**Fair Market Value (FMV)** — The price an asset would sell for between a willing buyer and seller in an open market.

**Four Pillars of Diversification** — A framework for spreading risk: geography, asset class, sponsor, and investment strategy.

**Fractional Ownership** — Owning a share of a property (as in a DST or Tenants-in-Common structure) rather than the entire property.

**Free and Clear** — Property owned without debt.

**Fund of Funds (FOF)** — Diversified portfolios of passive real estate deals where investor capital is pooled and then deployed across a curated mix of underlying deals. Aim is to reduce risk through sponsor and asset diversification, while still offering tax benefits and attractive projected return.

**Gain (Realized Gain)** — The profit realized on the sale of a property, calculated as Sale Price minus Adjusted Basis.

**General Partner (GP)** — The managing partner of a fund or syndication, typically responsible for acquisitions, financing, and operations.

**Grouping Election** — An IRS election allowing real estate professionals to combine multiple rental activities for material participation and passive loss rules.

**Holding Period** — The length of time an asset is owned before it is sold.

**Identification Period** — The 45-day window after selling a relinquished property in which a taxpayer must identify replacement properties.

**Installment Sale** — A sale where at least one payment is received after the tax year of the sale. May be combined with a 1031 strategy.

**Internal Rate of Return (IRR)** — The annualized rate of return earned on an investment, factoring in both cash flow and sale proceeds.

**Leverage** — The use of borrowed capital (debt) to increase potential returns on investment.

**Like-Kind Property** — Real estate held for investment or business use that qualifies for a 1031 exchange.

**Limited Partner (LP)** — A passive investor in a partnership or fund who has limited liability and no management control.

**Loan-to-Value Ratio (LTV)** — Loan Amount ÷ Property Value, expressed as a percentage.

**Management Company (MC)** — The entity responsible for day-to-day operations of a fund or property.

**Material Participation** — A tax test to determine whether a taxpayer actively participates in an activity, impacting passive loss rules.

**Mezzanine Debt** — A hybrid form of financing between senior debt and equity, often secured by an ownership interest.

**Net Operating Income (NOI)** — Income from property operations (rents and other income) minus operating expenses, before debt service and taxes.

**Non-Recourse Loan** — A loan secured only by the collateral property, not by the borrower's personal assets.

**Operating Partnership (OP) Units** — Interests received in an UPREIT structure in exchange for contributing property.

**Opportunity Cost** — Concept of time lost by self-managing investments rather than hiring others to handle investment activities. I.e., loss of potential gain from other alternatives when one alternative is chosen.

**Opportunity Zone (OZ)** — A federal program offering tax incentives for investing capital gains in designated distressed areas.

**Passive Activity Loss (PAL) Rules** — IRS rules limiting the use of losses from passive activities (such as rental real estate) to offset active income.

**Preferred Return** — A minimum annual return that must be paid to investors before profits are shared with the sponsor.

**Private Placement** — An investment offering exempt from SEC registration, typically limited to accredited investors.

**Promote Structure** — A share of profits above a set return.

**Qualified Intermediary (QI)** — A neutral third party who facilitates a 1031 exchange by holding sale proceeds and promotes compliance with IRS rules.

**Qualified Opportunity Fund (QOF)** — Investment vehicles for financially distressed areas known as opportunity zones, established by 2017 Tax Cuts and Jobs Act (TCJA) to boost investments in low-income or underdeveloped areas.

**Real Estate Investment Trust (REIT)** — Company that owns, operates, or finances income-producing real estate, allowing individuals to invest in large-scale properties (like malls, apartments, hospitals) without directly buying or managing them.

**Recapture** — See "Depreciation Recapture."

**Relinquished Property** — The property sold in a 1031 exchange.

**Replacement Property** — The property acquired in a 1031 exchange.

**Reverse Exchange** — A type of 1031 exchange where the replacement property is acquired before the relinquished property is sold.

**Safe Harbor Rules** — IRS guidelines that, if followed, protect taxpayers from disqualification of their exchange.

**Self-Directed IRA (SD-IRA)** — A retirement account that allows investment in real estate and other alternative assets.

**Sponsor / Asset Manager** — Sources deals, secures financing, hires property managers, and guides the investment

**Step Transaction Doctrine** — A tax principle that disallows transactions that technically comply with rules but are part of a larger scheme lacking substance.

**Step-Up in Basis** — Adjustment of an inherited property's basis to its fair market value at death, eliminating prior gains.

**Syndication** — A pooled investment structure where multiple investors combine capital to purchase property.

**Tenants-in-Common (TIC)** — A co-ownership structure where multiple investors each own a fractional, undivided interest in a property.

**Timeline (45/180 Rule)** — The dual deadlines in a 1031 exchange: 45 days to identify replacement property and 180 days to close.

**Treasury Yield Spread** — The difference in yields between two U.S. Treasury securities, often a proxy for market expectations.

**Umbrella Partnership REIT (UPREIT)** — A structure allowing property owners to contribute assets to a REIT in exchange for operating partnership units.

**Unrelated Business Taxable Income (UBTI)** — Income from certain investments in retirement accounts that may trigger tax liability.

**Waterfall (Distribution Waterfall)** — The order in which investment cash flows are distributed, typically prioritizing return of capital, then preferred returns, then profit splits.

**Withholding Tax (FIRPTA Withholding)** — Tax withheld on the sale of U.S. real property by foreign owners under the Foreign Investment in Real Property Tax Act.

For 1031 exchange guidance, visit https://1031x.com

To see if Passive Investing is right for you, choose your time to speak to one of Ironton Capital's investor relations team at https://irontoncapital.com/gopassive

# Appendix F: Index

For 1031 exchange guidance, visit https://1031x.com

To see if Passive Investing is right for you, choose your time to speak to one of Ironton Capital's investor relations team at https://irontoncapital.com/gopassive

Made in the USA
Coppell, TX
17 March 2026

73715341R00134